THE LIBERALS IN HAMPSHIRE –
a Part(l)y History

Part 1
Southampton 1958-65: object lessons

MARTIN KYRLE

In preparation:

Part 2 Chandler's Ford 1966-72: out in the suburbs,
     something stirred!

Part 3 Eastleigh 1972-80: the thorn in the side bursts
     into flower.

By the same author:

Martin Kyrle's *Little Green Nightbook* (see page 61)

In preparation:

Martin Kyrle's *Little Blue Nightbook*

© Martin Kyrle 2012

ISBN 978-0-9564701-7-1

Published by Sarsen Press, 22 Hyde St., Winchester, Hants SO23 7DR
Tel: (01962) 854281
Printed in the UK

CONTENTS

FOREWORD

Michael Meadowcroft
Liberal MP for Leeds West 1983-7

One thing is sure about Liberalism: the awareness that one is a Liberal is a life sentence! So many of us come to this realisation through a combination of factors. Occasionally it comes through reading Liberal tracts but more often it comes through anger at illiberal attitudes amongst the "establishment" – which happened to me – but, as with Martin Kyrle, it can come through osmosis, via a friendship with a dedicated local Liberal friend.

Too many of our colleagues lack confidence in their Liberal beliefs. Even when it is manifestly clear that what society desperately needs is a powerful dose of Liberal values our colleagues all too often turn tail. This cannot be said of Martin Kyrle! His record is exemplary, adding a key role in the "back room" to his sallies into the front line as a candidate and as party chair. Over the years Martin has underpinned the party organisation in ways which, alas, tend to be downgraded these days. His partnership with his wife Margaret as the "front line" politician until her sad death last year was remarkably successful, both personally and politically.

One of the benefits of contemporary memoirs is the reminder of an aspect of the era long since forgotten. One such is Martin's reference to THOR, the comprehensive organisational package for Liberals pioneered by John Wallbridge. It was sometimes satirised by colleagues who put more faith in improvisation than in painstaking record keeping and in structured campaign methodology, but there was no doubt that those local organisations capable of applying the great THOR to their election planning, benefited electorally.

The consistency of Liberalism in Eastleigh, and to some extent in Hampshire more generally, is an example to other areas where the party's success has ebbed and flowed. It is particularly commendable given that success was not first embedded there in 1962 in the Orpington days, during my time at Liberal Party HQ, but came somewhat later – and has continued ever since. Politics will inevitably be influenced by local personalities, but it is far healthier if it is founded in the persuasive promotion of values and principles.

Martin's memoirs provide a vivid record of the spirit of politics over fifty plus years, in particular the *joie-de-vivre* of the Grimond years. It is a splendid account of his life in Liberal politics, with many entertaining anecdotes. History is important, not least when the record also offers the opportunity for analysis. By and large, the socialist left has been more prolific in producing memoirs and it is splendid that Martin Kyrle has done his bit in redressing the balance.

I look forward to reading further instalments of his memoirs.

May 2012

PREFACE

MARTIN KYRLE joined the Liberals fresh out of university, primarily because the party supported proportional representation without which, in his opinion, no country is a true democracy no matter how many elections it has. As he explains, he saw no point in belonging to something unless one also took some interest in what it did, and little by little he got drawn into becoming a Liberal activist. Over half a century later, he still is.

It would be fair to describe most Southampton Liberal Party members in the days recounted in these pages as 'armchair activists'. Attending the Executive Committee was seen as an end in itself, not the means to one. Practical matters such as the collection of party subscriptions was viewed as a rather demeaning chore which they could not possibly be expected to lower themselves to do, and they looked with disdain on those other members who were prepared to get their hands dirty collecting money or knocking on doors during elections. They saw nothing incongruous in spending an evening once a month debating the finer points of party policy when there was no possibility of any of their ideas being implemented, and saw no reason to complement their debates by undertaking practical activity which might make implementation possible, e.g. by standing for election and getting elected (two different things).

Joining the Liberals at the end of the 1950s did not hold out any prospect whatever of electoral success or any sort of political career, but by turning away from hand-wringing and empty theorising and instead embracing hard practice Martin Kyrle ended up with an unexpectedly varied career despite never expecting – nor, indeed, planning – it. The election in 1972 of his wife, Margaret, as Eastleigh Borough Council's first-ever Liberal councillor and her second glass ceiling-breaking role in becoming Eastleigh's first-ever Liberal Mayor in 1984 propelled him into the public role of Mayor's Escort – only to go one better by becoming Mayor of Eastleigh himself in 1993. Never as a child having remotely entertained any expectations of anything out of the ordinary happening to him, he used to tell his Year 11 class in school that if someone had told him when he was their age that one day he'd have dinner with Lord Mountbatten, shake hands with the Queen, attend a Buckingham Palace Garden Party, attend an investiture (when his wife Margaret received her OBE) or become Mayor of his town he'd have scoffed at the suggestion. So he'd warn the youngsters that they shouldn't rule out unlikely things happening to them, not necessarily because of anything they did themselves but because of whom they married and what *they* did.

During twenty years on the council in Eastleigh he was variously Spokesman on Housing, Chairman of the Planning Committee, Chairman of the Local Area Committee, put in a total of forty years on school governing bodies and (for 12 years) was Chairman of Governors of the borough's special school for severely mentally handicapped children. With the money from his Mayor's Charity Appeal he set up the Arts & Youth Trust, which fifteen years on is still providing small grants to youth organisations or individual young people in the borough towards expenses incurred in pursuing youth activities and music, theatre and dance. His party roles include fighting four parliamentary elections in the 1970s and '80s (and securing second place in all of them), donkey's years as a branch officer – variously chairman, vice-chairman or secretary – and also spells as chairman of the Hampshire county party organisation and other offices such as being Group Secretary. Amongst what he routinely refers to as 'dog'sbody jobs' is personally collecting all the money from local businesses who advertise in *Focus*, which he began doing in Chandler's Ford in 1970 and which means that each year the branch publishes *Focus* at a profit. These hands-on, practical aspects of politics are absolutely essential to the party's health, progress and keeping things running, but generally go unacknowledged because they are 'back room' and attract neither limelight nor prestige.

This part(l)y history is offered to current members as a manual of instruction on how to achieve conspicuous failure or spectacular success. While considering those options, the wealth of asides, observations, analysis and anecdotes leavening the lump mean that this book should be read sitting down, in case you laugh so much you fall over and do yourself a mischief.

A PART(L)Y HISTORY

PART I – 1958-65

'Isn't it time you joined the party?', asked John.
'Which party?' I replied.
'The Liberal Party.'
'How do you know I'm a Liberal?'
'I've known you for the past four years.'

JOINING THE PARTY

John Wallbridge was a fellow student at Southampton University but older than most, married and with a young family. I met him almost as soon as I went up in 1954 as he was chairman of the University Operatic Society, which I joined on the basis of having taken up singing in the sixth form at school, joined my music master's church choir at St Mary's in Portsea and then been in the chorus of Sittingbourne Operatic Society's production of *'Ruddigore'* when I was stationed at Chatham Barracks during my national service undergoing training as a cypher officer. John and I went on to do two Gilbert & Sullivan productions together, me progressing from chorus (*'HMS Pinafore'*) to tenor soloist *(*Col Fairfax in *'The Yeomen of the Guard'* and Cox in *'Cox and Box'),* and after he'd gone down I moved across to produce *'Patience'*. John also edited the undergraduate paper 'Wessex News', and took me on as a staffer.

Anecdote No 1
There were university Conservative and Labour Clubs, but no Liberal equivalent. Despite having only a handful of members, the Labour Club felt it their duty to show their opposition to alleged

1

atrocities in prison camps in East Africa where locals demanding independence were being detained.

They decided to stage a demonstration in the main shopping street in the middle of the town, and at a pre-arranged signal their leader stepped into the road with his banner, followed by the others.

They were not best pleased with my report in Wessex News: 'All five members of the Labour Club staged a mass demonstration in Above Bar against British atrocities in Kenya'.

One day, lacking any real 'news', he had an idea to create a story to fill up the empty space. Having noticed a temporary bus stop in The Avenue (the main road from Southampton northwards), he proposed to the editorial team that we should transport it to Stonehenge in his dormobile, stand it among the stones and then take photographs of our backsides as we all prostrated ourselves before it as if worshipping an idol. We then took it back to Southampton, and replaced it *in situ*. Sounds daft, but that was the sort of harmless stunt students got up to in those days. I also worked with John in the Rag Show, where I sang in the chorus line and did a conjuring act. He was in many ways my mentor during my first years as an undergraduate, and though at the time I knew nothing of his political affiliations and, indeed, was not interested in politics, it was hardly surprising that when he invited me to join his party I did so without much hesitation. I had no idea that Liberal politics would be a dominant feature of the rest of my life.

John owned a scruffy post-First World War house in Freemantle, a run-down part of Southampton, and when I graduated and enrolled to do a PGCE (Post-graduate Certificate in Education) I rented it from him. He left it to me to find three other young men to share it to keep our costs down, but emphasised that I was the tenant with responsibility for seeing that the rent was paid and by implication for the proper running of the household. 'I'm not having you fathering children on my springs' was the warning he gave me with regard to how we were expected to conduct ourselves. Lively student parties, fine. But he wouldn't be agreeable to us putting a red light outside the front door and running a brothel. Luckily, my friends and I had no intention of doing that anyway.

After completing my PGCE I moved across town to Portswood and shared a one-room flat at the upstairs back of a large Victorian house in Alma Road with adjoining kitchen and bathroom with a fellow graduate, Cliff Eveleigh. Cliff had read English, and although like me he had done a PGCE and got his first teaching post he wanted to move into banking and had ambitions to become a writer. He had a 'serious' girlfriend, Dawn, also a recent Southampton graduate, and when they wanted a bit of privacy (we referred to it as 'nesting'), I would make myself scarce and go out with my own girlfriend to the pictures or whatever and leave them in peace. We lived in that close proximity for a year without ever having a cross word, and I was devastated when two years later and having only just got married, he died, aged 26, of lung cancer – never having smoked in his life.

My next move was to another large Victorian house but in the next road, Gordon Avenue, where I rented a single room on the ground floor with a tiny kitchen and lavatory, but my own private back door so that I could come and go as I pleased and alongside which I could park my motorbike away from the road. Independent living at last!

John's brother-in-law Nicko had been a fellow student with me, indeed we'd both taken part in Op Soc productions, and he lived a mile or so away in Highfield with his wife, Jean, John's sister; I knew them well and frequently popped in for coffee and a chat. I happened to be there when John came to visit, and that's when the conversation at the head of this chapter took place. I suspect John picked his time to approach me, well aware that not many people would consider joining a party which barely existed outside the West Country and some rural parts of Wales and Scotland, had

3

barely half-a-dozen MPs, failed to put up candidates in most parliamentary constituencies and lost its deposit in most of those where it did. He must have reasoned that the period in my early adult life dominated by study, exams and gaining qualifications and my leisure time taken up with operatic society productions and seeking the company of clever, pretty girls was now over, and that I had moved on from the student world into the world of work, career and paying taxes and was also now living a bachelor life on my own. If he wanted to recruit me into his party, now was the optimum point to tempt me into taking up a new interest. He gave me a booklet summarising party policy, and what attracted my eye most of all was the clear and unequivocal commitment to proportional representation, which I had long thought was essential in a functioning democracy. That policy on its own was enough to persuade me to join and, as I still maintain my view that while first-past-the-post is a wonderful way to decide who wins a horse race or an Olympic sprint but is not an appropriate tool if what you are trying to create is a representative body whose members are elected, my attachment to the Liberal Party under its various subsequent names has never wavered.

EARLY POLITICS

In taking any interest in politics, let alone joining a party, I was breaking new ground. In my family everyone claimed, if asked, to be a member of the Church of England but never went to church, not even at Christmas or Easter. Everyone claimed to vote Conservative because that was what respectable people were supposed to do, but without ever joining the party or for that matter, ever having a sensible discussion about politics. To vote for the alternative – Labour – would be lining oneself up with the working classes alongside bolshies, people who criticised the Royal Family or Mr Churchill, assorted vagabonds, guttersnipes and conchies and was unthinkable. Of course, none of my family knew anything about politics, or cared. It was a toffee-nosed 'class' thing. Despite being poor as church mice they all thought themselves better than their neighbours, and voting Conservative was how they demonstrated that they were not working class like them but middle class – the class above them. Whether their unthinking support for the Tories ever translated into actually walking down to the village, going into a polling station and putting a cross on a ballot paper, I rather doubt. I certainly never remember any one of them ever voting. Their 'support' for the Conservatives was probably as valuable to the local Tory MP as their adherence to the C of E was to the vicar. When in my early teens I was sent off to Sunday School, it was to the one held in the nearest ecclesiastical building – the local Methodist Church Hall – not to the Anglican church in the village a mile away across the fields.

In taking no interest in politics, parties or who was the local MP or member of the local council my family back in the '40s and '50s was not unique but pretty much the norm, at least in rural areas such as the one I grew up in. Despite their snobbish pretensions based merely on working in offices or being housewives who didn't go to work at all, when judged on the basis of their level of education, incomes and seniority at their places of work my family were all working class. Working class people such as they didn't think it was their place to take an interest in politics, which they viewed as something for people higher up the social scale to bother themselves with, a sort of 'let our betters decide and tell us who to vote for, and we'll go and vote for them' – though, as just observed, out of basic indolence they never actually did it. There was still this idea of respectability by association – if the respectable middle classes vote Conservative and we do too, then we are a bit more respectable and a bit more middle class than we would be if we didn't. Political infantilism was pathetic then, but at least it could be partly excused by the absence of a rounded education, exacerbated by the fact that for their generation what education there was ceased to be compulsory at the age of twelve. No one nowadays has any excuse, but the phenomenon is still all too prevalent – ask anyone who's ever gone canvassing at an election.

My knowledge of practical politics may have been nil, but from studying history in the sixth form at school I knew a great deal about the theory, about parties and about how they operated in government. Five years of dictated notes on the period 1815-1914 meant I could explain in quite unnecessary detail the rivalry between Gladstone and Disraeli and recite the provisions of the Reform Acts of 1832 and 1867 from memory – literally, as that was the way history was taught in my school: you learned it all by heart and got regularly tested on it. But what interest would anyone have in voting when doing so would make no difference? As a child I lived in Clanfield, a village just off the main London road twelve miles out of Portsmouth and five miles from the market town of Petersfield in a parliamentary constituency where, as the cliché goes, they didn't count the Tory vote at elections, they weighed it. When the result was a foregone conclusion, why should anyone bother to cast their vote? Not that I had one, of course, in the days when enfranchisement took place at 21. At that age I was in Malta doing my national service in the Royal Navy, and no one in authority ever suggested that I was entitled to a postal vote or how I should go about getting one – even if I'd been interested.

During my undergraduate days I lived in a university hall of residence, and never remember any political literature ever being distributed. I suppose Southampton's political parties assumed that most undergraduates were too young to vote and any who did would vote at home, not in Southampton. There were council elections, but no one ever seems to have twigged that although most students were up straight from school there was a fair sprinkling of ex-national servicemen such as myself who were over 21 and who could have been persuaded to have their names put on the electoral roll if anyone had ever bothered to suggest it. But no party activists did that, nor, for that matter, did the university authorities ever acknowledge a duty to remind us that as adult citizens we had a vote and ought to use it when opportunity offered. Connaught and the other halls of residence existed in an electoral no-man's-land.

The vote I do remember from my days in Connaught was the election held during my first term for a 'Freshers' Rep', i.e. a first-year student to sit on the management committee which ran our hall of residence. I supported the candidature of a friend, Vaughan Arnold, and on his behalf canvassed other first years. However, when nominations closed we found that one of them had noted – as one does – that there had never been anyone on the Hall Committee who came from Hitchin *(where?)*. That was where he came from, and he thought it would be nice to have someone from Hitchin on the committee and had got the two other freshers who came from that area to nominate him. Why on earth candidates for election to a student hall committee should be supported on the basis of which run-of-the-mill provincial town they came from has never been apparent to me, but his intervention was crucial as he got, predictably, three votes, my friend Vaughan got seven and lost by one to the other chap who secured eight. What got my goat was that the 'Hitchin' candidate had been one of those I'd approached on Vaughan's behalf and who'd promised his support before deciding that it was vital for our hall committee to have the benefit of a member from Hitchin and had put himself up instead. However, with hindsight I regard this as the beginnings of my commitment to PR. The winner of the election got eight votes, but there were ten votes cast against him. It didn't seem quite right to me then, and in later years as I grew more politically astute I realised why. There was something inherently spurious in someone claiming to 'represent' a group of people when the majority of them had voted against him. So the winner's claim to 'represent' everyone was bogus – a pretence. That still applies to most members of the House of Commons as it always has, and is the basis of my long-held view that although my country has elections it is not a democracy.

MY FIRST VOTE

It was not until I'd moved out of Connaught and into the rented house in Freemantle that I voted for the first time in a party political election. I remember the occasion well. In the May 1958 council elections we got a leaflet through our front door from the Labour candidate, one A.G. Steavenson. There was no indication as to what 'A.G.' stood for – presumably 'none of your business, and don't start getting familiar with *me*!' It bore a photograph of a heavily-jowled, balding man described as 'in his fifties' and looking as if he was seriously over-weight. It then gave it to us electors straight: 'You and your family need A.G. Steavenson on the council'. My reactions to this assertion were: one, who the hell do they think they are to tell me who I *need*? That's for me to decide, not you; and second, me and my family certainly don't need A.G. Steavenson on the council or, for that matter, anywhere else (on the moon, perhaps?) as being a single man, I haven't got one. The Tory candidate, Tom Eccles, seemed from his literature harmless enough, so I voted for him just to spite A.G. Steavenson. If he hadn't tried to patronise me I wouldn't have bothered to vote at all, but by doing so he had so riled me that I'd gone to the polling station *for the first time in my life* solely to demonstrate my irritation by casting my vote for the other candidate.

THE SOUTHAMPTON LIBERAL ASSOCIATION

Following John Wallbridge's urging, in November of that year – 1958 – I paid my first membership subscription to the local Liberal Association, as they were called in those days, and went to my first meeting – what's the point of joining something if you don't then take some part in what it does? It was a bit of a culture shock. I was 25, there was another member, Ken Makepeace, who was about 40, and the rest were either elderly middle-aged or so far advanced in years as to be positively decrepit. Total party membership for the entire city was in low double figures, and most paid-up members did nothing except pay the required annual sub of half-a-crown if someone bothered to come round to collect it *[NB to modern readers: that's 12½p – a year! Think what kind of vibrant national organisation the Liberals were able to run on that!]*. Any member who wanted to take any sort of active part was automatically on the Executive, which numbered about ten. The party Executive was, therefore, self-appointed, and consisted of any paid-up party member who had the time or inclination to sit on it. The pitfalls of this arrangement became more apparent as time went on, as will be unfolded as our narrative makes its stately progress.

It – the Executive committee – met once a month in the basement of the offices of B.F. Tite, an architectural practice located in Carlton Crescent, in the Georgian part of Southampton. Basil Tite was the party secretary, and like many Liberals in those days a practising Methodist. He was also an extremely nice man, and with resigned good humour did his best to cajole the committee members at meetings to stick to the agenda and to talk sense. He usually cajoled in vain.

Ken Makepeace alone had some idea what the Liberal Association's aims should be, i.e. it existed to gain the support of the public for liberal policies and the way to do this was to put up candidates for the city council and the House of Commons, and that to do this we needed a regular income of some sort. Without a commitment to supporting candidates at elections we were merely a debating society rather than a functioning part of a national political party. He himself campaigned for our candidate in Millbrook. The Liberal vote steadily increased and peaked in 1962 with a stunning second place. Putting one's money where one's mouth was was not, in those days, a cliché as anyone brave enough (foolhardy? committed?) to stand for election had to pay their own expenses. The Association had insufficient funds to do so.

Funds. That was a major problem. The lack of them, bordering on total absence, or any serious ideas – or even the will – for improving them. Ken proposed a 'shilling-a-month' scheme *[NB = 5p]*. He would knock on someone's door and announce boldly

'My name is Mr Makepeace', emphasising each word with equal force, which I reckoned would have put the wind up a lot of people answering their door, especially as he was about six feet tall. He would then collect a shilling off them for the party funds. How cost-effective this would be once one had factored in the time it would take him in the hours available after he'd finished work for the day set against the number of shillings the Association would be the richer by at the end of a month was not debated, nor what would happen if it rained a lot or he took a holiday or was ill. However, he had the right idea: without regular income, the party would never be able to plan ahead and would never get anywhere. None of the others had any better suggestions – nor, incidentally, any intention of getting up off their backsides and following Ken's example.

Apart from donations, including Basil's donation in kind by having our meetings on his premises without charging for heat and light, our income came from two sources: membership subscriptions and a summer garden party. This was held in the grounds of an imposing residence in Abbott's Way in the more affluent part of Highfield not far from the university, owned by a pair of elderly spinster sisters, the Misses Grassam Sims, staunch, lifelong Liberals since their childhood in Victorian times, who graciously allowed us the use of their large garden. They themselves declined to make a personal appearance, and it's strange that despite attending the event for several years I never once saw, let alone met, either of them even though they were at home.

George Payne, our regular candidate in St Luke's ward, paid his election expenses each year out of the accumulated profits of weekly Friday night whist drives in the local scout hut organised by his wife. I enjoyed a hand of whist, so often went along as the hut was walking distance from my flat. Most of the patrons were old people from the neighbourhood who all voted for George because of his wife, and prizes consisted of tins of meat, pots of jam, fresh vegetables (e.g. a large cabbage or a bunch of carrots), half-a-dozen eggs and other cheap-and-cheerful everyday household staples. She ran it like a Roman war galley, possibly drawing her inspiration from her wartime service in the WRNS. At the end of each hand she clapped her hands – chop-chop!, no shilly-shallying! – and we changed tables at something approaching ramming speed (v. *Ben Hur*), sat down and started dealing the next hands. She stopped at the halfway point to draw the raffle and serve refreshments: tea and biscuits – or for bearded intellectuals such as myself, coffee, which came out of a bottle; older readers may remember a popular liquid brand called 'Camp', which bore a label depicting an Indian Army officer in full Highland dress enjoying his cup, with his native Indian batman standing by with a tray, ready to pour a refill. At the end, prizes were awarded for highest-scoring man and woman against a background of polite but scattered applause and the scraping of chairs and general hubbub as people got up to go home. *But she made a profit*, out of which she funded her husband's idiosyncratic hobby of standing for the council each year and always coming third with 300 votes or thereabouts (10%) and a thousand votes behind the other two parties. Her profits also paid for the hire of a coach in summer to take the old folk for a day-out at the seaside, and a visit to the panto at Christmas. Looking back, I now realise that without any reference or deference to the Constituency Association she was running in a totally unpretentious manner a branch which, be it noted, met the four criteria which any branch claiming to be successful has to achieve: to be solvent, self-sufficient, have a social programme and without fail put up a candidate at each election. Dare one suggest that St Luke's Ward in the late '50s and early '60s was possibly by half-a-century ahead of some of our local branches at the present time?

Then someone came up with a brand new suggestion for raising money: why don't we run a jumble sale?

We had two old biddies who regularly attended the Executive, bringing to its deliberations a blissful, complacent ignorance of politics coupled with decided prejudices about everything – basically, if it was a new idea, they were agin' it. They were active members of the Liberal Party if by that you mean that once a month they got on a bus and attended the Executive. They never did anything else. They represented no one but themselves because, as already explained, anyone prepared to come to the Executive was automatically on it. Woe betide any other member present who questioned their right to be there or who queried the value of their contributions to discussion! It appeared that the Almighty in His wisdom had put them on earth with instructions to devote their lives to obstructing the local Liberal Association in every way possible, and secure two aims: (1) it was totally ineffective; and (2) it stayed that way. People of this stripe had on the one hand kept the Liberal Party alive since the War, but at the same time, on the other hand, they'd killed it.

Eventually they were persuaded, largely through Basil's quiet assurances, that this newfangled idea of a jumble sale would not compromise their Christian principles (more Methodism) or start us on a slippery slope (leading, perhaps, to *solvency*?). But when it came to deciding the price we should charge the public for admission they argued like Kilkenny cats for twenty minutes, voices raised, shouting at each other across the table, as to whether it should be tuppence or thre'pence (2d or 3d; in decimal, 1p or 1½p). You can only imagine what I made of this display of elderly affronted outrage and lack of self-control. Put yourself in my place: 26, fresh out of university with a good degree in History, attending the party Executive expecting serious, adult discussion about ways and means of advancing liberal principles and prepared to get my hands dirty raising money as a necessary chore if it would help fund the elections which were the primary purpose of the Association, now witnessing two elderly ladies who ought to know better having a shouting match across a table in front of the rest of us and almost tearing each other's hair out over the difference of one penny for admission at the door. It was absolutely unbelievable – except that I was present so it *was* believable! We eventually agreed on thre'pence, for the purely practical reason that a threepenny bit was a single coin so easier to collect, and also weighed a lot less than two pennies. I added that lots of people would come as couples, husband and wife, and could pay with another single coin, a sixpence, whereas if we were charging 2d each they'd probably give us four pennies – so more time and trouble to count and more weight to carry home and then take to the bank the following week. However, trying to work in a committee with these two silly, self-opinionated and proudly ignorant old fools taught me lessons which I have frequently drawn on throughout my political life, as will be revealed when describing other events elsewhere many years later.

I did my PGCE teaching practice at King Edward VI School in Southampton during the spring term of 1958, where my supervisor was the Head of History, T.C. Stanley-Little. His lessons, which I 'observed', were a master class in how not to do it. He couldn't maintain order and discipline (in a grammar school!), and his lessons were utterly chaotic with boys throwing paper darts and rubbers about and shouting and him shouting back, demanding their names and writing them down on scraps of paper but, as the boys knew perfectly well, never following up with any punishment (NB: he taught the same classes week after week, yet didn't appear to know any of the boys' names). When I attended my next meeting in Basil's basement, who should I find there but 'T.C.' – unbeknown to me our previous parliamentary candidate for Southampton Test and now taking an interest in order to be re-adopted (he lived in the New Forest somewhere near New Milton). He had more the character and mind-set of an early nineteenth century Whig than a modern Liberal, and because I'd seen him in action in school and knew how ineffectual he was I couldn't see him as a serious parliamentary candidate.

The results in Southampton Test in 1955 had been:

J.M. Howard	Conservative	26 707	51.2%
C.A.R. Crosland	Labour	22 865	43.8%
T.C. Stanley-Little	Liberal	2 583	5.0%

Conservative majority 3 842

There had been no Liberal candidate for Test at the previous election in 1951, when Labour's Dr Horace King, subsequently Speaker of the House of Commons, held on by only 465 votes. The situation in the other Southampton seat, Itchen, was from a Liberal point of view even worse: no candidate was fielded between 1950 and 1964. The problem for the Association was that although 'T.C' had lost his deposit he had not lost his conviction that the enthusiastic endorsement of two-and-a-half thousand electors entitled him to automatic nomination for the next election, scheduled for later that year. There was a fearsome row when the committee refused to re-adopt him, and he responded by putting a letter in the local paper, *The Echo,* calling upon all true Liberals (!) to dissociate themselves from the renegades running the local Association and join *him,* the standard-bearer of real Liberalism. The equivalent of 'It's my bat and my ball, and if I can't have it all my own way I'll take them home.' Unfortunately, this attitude is not unknown in political parties in times long since, as many readers of this volume will doubtless attest with a raising of the eyebrows and a glance skywards in recollection.

The difficulty in those days of finding candidates was even more marked when it came to parliamentary elections, where a lost deposit was the norm and local Associations who could barely afford a one-leaflet campaign were quite unable to produce a cash deposit – and it had to *be* cash, cheques were not accepted – let alone lose it. As a result many candidates were endorsed simply because they offered to pay for their own campaign and put up their own deposit, regardless of the obvious fact that as aspirants to membership of the House of Commons they were totally unsuitable. The prevailing view was that any candidate no matter how flawed was better than no candidate at all, and the mouths of gift horses were not looked in, so to speak. But seeing some of the Grade I Listed buffoons who were officially endorsed as Liberal candidates in the days of endemic party weakness made me doubt the wisdom of this view. If you want your party to be taken seriously, this won't happen if its public face, i.e. its candidate, is a twerp.

As a teacher employed by the city council, I was ineligible to serve as a councillor. I decided therefore that I would instead devote myself to the engine room rather than the bridge: I'd learn how to be an agent. Liberal Party HQ offered a postal agent's course, sending large envelopes full of information for the would-be agent to master, together with an accompanying question paper which he was expected to fill in and post back for marking. On successfully completing this course of study the Chief Agent reckoned that you knew enough about being an election agent at least to keep both yourself and your candidate out of jail, and I was pleasantly (self) satisfied when some months later he awarded me 99%. Long after, it occurred to me that a missing element in this training was an oral examination, or at least a face-to-face interview, to discover how as Agent you would deal with conflict within the Association or react in a crisis or under fire, to ascertain whether, as well as being pretty good at filling in nomination papers and submitting your return of election expenses on time, having several fillings missing from your front teeth, industrial-strength halitosis and habitually three days' growth of stubble (particularly if you were a woman) might on occasion militate against your effectiveness in promoting your candidate. Passing a correspondence course without any supervision was very obviously open to fraud, and even if a candidate genuinely absorbed the regulations there's a bit more to the job than that. Being a successful agent also requires 'people skills' and an equable temperament – the ability to keep a cool head and not panic when, for example, you discover that the opposition candidate met yours in the street and said "Boo!" and your Association chairman has just announced to the press that he intends to issue a writ.

THOR

John Wallbridge had realised that the party's lack of electoral success was in large measure due to a total lack of recognition of the fundamentals of political organisation, and that no training in such skills was offered. Election campaigns for the council comprised delivery of an election address, and the candidate with the help of such members as could be persuaded to risk it knocking on as many doors as they could in the three weeks prior to polling day. Tellers may have sat at a few polling stations taking numbers, but if these were collected and taken back to the committee room no one knew what to do with them and they just piled up on a table. A parliamentary election was the same only on a larger scale, with the addition of a series of public meetings where the candidate declaimed party policy and took questions. Attendance varied, from the party faithful listening in awe to someone who appeared to know what party policy actually was, those where occasionally a member of the opposition turned up to try to disrupt the proceedings and generally take the piss, to those where no one turned up except the candidate and his agent and half an hour was spent thumb-twiddling while the caretaker continually shifted on his feet and glared at his watch. It doesn't require much training to be able to run such a campaign: hire a hall, stick up a few posters and put a brief announcement in the local paper, print an election address and go out and deliver it (by yourself, most of the time). But neither was it particularly effective. The modern concepts of identifying your supporters and where they live, concentrating on polling day on getting them to go out and vote and then at other times of the year outside elections having a programme of systematic recruitment or delivering to the public any kind of party leaflet unconnected with an imminent election did not exist back then.

John had decided to do something practical about this. He devised a whole spectrum of task-specific forms: for recording who'd voted, forms for use in the committee room to enable us to score out those who had and then go out and knock up those who hadn't, forms for passing on to other constituencies details of a member who'd moved to their territory, forms for keeping a record of supporters, forms for recording party members and when their subs were due, forms with tick-lists of equipment essential in the committee room to ensure it was all in place and anything superfluous was removed, and so on. He dubbed this organisation organisation *(not a misprint – try reading it again)* THOR. And no – I don't know why, either.

He posed fundamental questions, and proposed answers or suggested solutions. Should you have a committee room on election day, and if so what should be in it, who, and what should they be doing? What, fundamentally, was canvassing *for*? There was, for example, the school of thought that you stuck your foot in the door and refused to leave until the householder had agreed to vote Liberal. No amount of pointing out that such promises obtained under duress were worthless made any impact on the absolute certainty with which this view of door-to-door canvassing was held by some people. Might work selling cleaning materials from an open basket to harassed housewives – not sure it works with getting people to go to a polling station in a fortnight's time and keep a promise to vote for you which had been made as the only way to get you off their doorstep and your jabbing forefinger out of the middle of their chest. Other members not only refused to canvass but into the bargain expressed moral disapproval of those who did, telling us that such behaviour was an unpardonable intrusion into people's privacy and as such wasn't really *Liberal*. Those who did agree to knock on doors often had no idea how to record the results, blithely putting down everyone who said 'I'll think about it' as a 'possible' to be reminded on polling day.

To provide this training, John invited volunteers to come to his house at Southborough, between Tonbridge and Tunbridge Wells, for a 'Liberal week-end'. We took our own sleeping bags, and most of us ended up on the floor – men in one room, women in another. One of our party was James Woodward-Nutt, who had been a fellow student at Southampton and although not a member of Op Soc had fallen under John Wallbridge's sway through being in the same Hall of Residence. He told me many years later that he'd jocularly asked for a bedroom with a bathroom *en suite* – and found he'd been given a bed in the bathroom (which one could argue was what he'd asked for). There was a great deal of '*nudge, nudge, wink, wink*' from our friends when I went off with my girlfriend, Margaret, for a 'Liberal weekend', but the fact was there was neither opportunity nor time for any intimacy. We arrived on Friday night, and on Saturday morning after a communal breakfast had a lecture on the topic of the day. Under the title of 'Canvassing' there would be in-depth discussion and analysis of baseline fundamentals, e.g. what was canvassing actually *for* (i.e. why do we bother to do it in the first place?). Then, how to react when the door's opened, what to ask, how long to spend with each elector (including how to disengage from timewasters or the clinically insane) and – most importantly of all – what to record on your canvass card when you'd finished. In the evening we went off door-knocking to try putting the theory into practice, and next morning went through our experiences and assessed how we'd done and what we'd learned of the practicalities of calling on members of the public in their own homes to enquire about their voting intentions and were they disposed to vote Liberal. John, as his part of the bargain, got a large chunk of his ward canvassed by enthusiastic young people – and his candidate won it at the next local election.

John adhered to a Spartan, utilitarian concept of committee rooms: they were places where vital work was done on election day, not gossip chambers for tired knockers-up to clog up, milling around drinking coffee and distracting other workers with reminiscences about their adventures that morning – or even worse, their adventures at the last election or 'back in 19..'. He justified this by telling us of one recent election where we'd failed to win the seat by seven votes, and there were nine Liberal workers in the committee room who, when pressed, all admitted that despite having spent most of the day knocking up and asking our supporters to get down to the polling station and cast their vote had neglected to do it themselves. On this basis, he ordained that knockers-up or returning tellers should on no account be admitted into the committee room and their reports or papers handed over in the doorway and they then be shown into a different room where they could rest, drink tea and reminisce to their hearts' content but without interfering with the other polling day workers 'eyes down' in the committee room. In one election as Agent in St Luke's Ward in Southampton I took this to extremes. Our committee room was in a house which had a window opening directly onto the pavement. We told all knockers-up to collect their knocking-up lists through this window, and all tellers to hand their telling slips in likewise – with the result that none of them even set foot in the committee room. Via the front door they had access to the rest of the house, the kitchen was at their disposal, refreshment freely available and armchairs and sofas in the front room allowed them to take a break in comfort. But the door to the committee room remained resolutely locked on the inside, thus preventing cheery visitors and well-wishers swanning in to regale us with their latest anecdotes or 'When I was in Sidi Barani'. It didn't win us the seat, but I'm sure it maximised our vote.

Anecdote No 2.
On one of these 'Liberal weekends' I was out canvassing with Jim Woodward-Nutt. I was at the front door of the end house of a row, having just canvassed the occupant. Jim was next door, at a house which was very deep from front to back, the rear more or less level with me, the front of the house projecting some forty feet behind me.

The house was in total darkness. It was half past seven, so it would be sensible to assume that the occupants were out. But we'd been taught not to make any assumptions, so Jim rang the doorbell. From where I was standing I saw a light come on upstairs, right at the back. Then another and another, as whoever-it-was worked his or her way down the stairs, along corridors and through various rooms, switching on lights each time all the way through the house from the upstairs back to the downstairs front, to answer the door. It must have taken about ten minutes, Jim ringing a second time and all the while standing patiently at the front of the house waiting to see if anyone was going to come to the door, but unsighted so quite unaware of the lightshow visible to me standing outside the neighbouring house. It opened to reveal an elderly lady in her dressing gown. 'Good evening. I'm from the local Liberals,' said Jim. 'Will you be voting for us at the next election?', or words from our instruction script to that effect. Pause. Then in a piping, almost whining voice, rising in pitch and volume as she reached the end of the sentence, the old lady responded: 'We was in bed!' – and shut the door in his face. I've no doubt Jim recorded this correctly as 'Not Voting'.

Anecdote No 3.
The following exchange also took place in the course of a 'Liberal weekend'.

'Good evening', I said to the rather large, dishevelled man who answered my knock. 'I'm from the local Liberals. Are you likely to vote for us at the next election?'

'I'll have you know I'm the local Labour councillor. You're wasting your time round here', came the firm and rather truculent response.

'Well, you're the first person who's said so', I replied pleasantly, and moved off, leaving him with his mouth still open.

And lo! It came to pass that at the next local elections, verily he did lose his seat.

MY FIRST PARLIAMENTARY ELECTION

[Historical note on Liberal parliamentary candidates in Southampton. Group Capt. R. Fulljames was Liberal candidate in 1945, when the city was one seat. It was split into Itchen and Test in 1950, but other than Stanley-Little in 1955 no Liberal stood in Test until 1966. In 1950 Itchen was fought by S. Fry, but there was no subsequent Liberal there until Jo Cherryson in 1964. Labour's Dr Horace King, previously MP for Test but fearful of losing what had become a marginal seat, moved across to Itchen, became Speaker of the House of Commons and was not opposed by the other main parties in the 1966 and 1970 elections. He did not seek re-election in 1974, thus allowing Jo to stand again in both February and October. From that election on, and in Test from 1966, there have always been Liberal, SDP, Alliance or Liberal Democrat candidates at general elections].

As we had no candidate in either Southampton seat in 1959, I went off to help John Wallbridge, who was Agent for Ruislip Northwood and had asked all THOR members not otherwise campaigning in their own constituencies to come if they could and get some hands-on experience at a parliamentary election. Our candidate's name was Walker, and our campaign slogan was 'Win With Walker!' Fat chance, but it scanned well.

Anecdote No 4
One of the first social events I organised for Portswood and St Luke's Liberals was a branch dinner at – wait for it! – the Chinese Restaurant. Note 'the', not 'a' or 'the local'. It was the first one in Southampton. Ordinary people were apprehensive about going there because they expected they'd be served a plate of dragon-on-toast which they'd have to eat sideways with a chopstick in each hand. It shows how different the world was back then, compared with nowadays when we have Chinese and Indian restaurants and takeaways sprinkled throughout our towns and cities and even

*located in villages and making a good living from the yokels whose
taste buds are nowadays more discerning.*

*My introduction to the pleasures of Chinese cuisine I lay
at John Wallbridge's door. Taking a break from tramping the
doorknockers of Ruislip, he took a cohort of us worker-ants to a
Chinese restaurant, sat us all round a large table and ordered up a
veritable cornucopia of god-know's-what, some of it possibly still
alive. Us provincials had never been inside such an establishment
and hadn't the slightest idea what any of the dishes were.*

*John, who serendipitously had been born in China where
his parents were missionaries, was completely at ease in front
of such a laden table, and to emphasise his complete mastery
of the situation picked up his pair of chopsticks and showed us
how to hold them (remember your first time? – and I am talking
about eating Chinese food). Then, in a superb exhibition of one-
upmanship, he reached across at arm's length to the middle of the
table and with the points of his chopsticks picked up a single pea
and reached back to put it into his mouth.*

Follow that!

The Conservative majority in 1955 in Ruislip Northwood had been
11,555, and our real objective was to save our deposit. *[In those
days, £150 – a lot of money! – and you lost it unless you polled
12½% of the votes cast].* The Labour candidate's name was Les
King, and he campaigned under the slogan 'Vote for King, the Man
with a Plan'. The press somehow set up photo-calls with all three
candidates with pints of beer in their hands, trying to demonstrate
to the public that behind all the electioneering they were all men of
the people, 'one of us' and on jolly good friendly terms with their
political opponents. Total baloney.

At that time many British colonies, especially in Africa, were
spawning independence movements, and the Government was
attempting to put them down by the use of armed force. One
Tory election meeting I attended showed them in a particularly

unpleasant light – a lesson not lost on me. The chairman, who wore very thick glasses, was boasting that 'I was very expensively educated, and I learned nothing at all!', his voice rising an octave as he practically shouted the final four words. How this was supposed to influence members of the audience to vote for Petre Crowder, the Tory candidate, I still haven't managed to work out. The atmosphere degenerated when the candidate started to give us his views on the uprising at that time going on in Kenya. There had been stories in the press about mistreatment of detainees by the British in various holding camps, the most notorious of which was called Hola. One of our group started to heckle, shouting 'Hola! Hola!' The Tory stewards grabbed him with much more physical force than was necessary, and bundled him outside. When someone in the front of the audience asked the chairman what action he proposed to take he replied that he'd seen it all clearly and our chap had struck the first blow so the stewards' strong-arm tactics were both justified and necessary as they were acting in self-defence. The fact was, our chap hadn't struck a blow at all, let alone the first – I know, because I was standing next to him. The other reason I didn't believe the chairman's confident declaration that he'd seen everything was that a man wearing bottle-glass specs couldn't possibly have seen from the platform at the front of the hall what was going on at the back. It was instructive to see proof that someone who sees himself as eminently respectable – by gad, Sir, he's chairman of the local Tory Party, what? – can reveal himself to be a brazen liar when it suits him.

On the subject of lies:

Anecdote No 5
In an effort to undermine our vote, the Labour camp took to describing King as 'the Liberal Labour candidate' – though whether that was 'Liberal' with a capital or a small 'l' is not clear, as they didn't put it on leaflets but said it over loudspeakers on vans going round and round the town centre.

I was standing at the roadside, wearing my green rosette, about to cross the road on my way back to our committee room when I heard approaching one of their loudspeaker vans proclaiming 'Vote for King – the liberal Labour candidate!'. The van stopped right alongside me – I was inadvertently standing outside the flight of steps which led up to Labour's HQ on the first floor. The driver, memorable for the fact that he had thick black eyebrows which met in the middle, got out and went to push past me (the rosette, I suppose).

'What's that you were saying over your loudspeaker?', I asked.

His face contorted with rage. 'You're a liar!', he bawled in my face, and rushed up the stairs.

No one has ever explained to me how you can call someone who asks a question a liar – surely you can only do that if they make a statement. The grammatical incongruity of that momentary exchange rooted the incident indelibly in my memory, accompanied as it was by a verbal assault at close quarters.

It also ensured that for the rest of my life I'd be totally immune to blandishments from Labour or invitations to vote for them – even less to join their party. That single angry and nonsensical accusation from a Labour activist ensured that I'd never, ever, be tempted to make common cause with a party which had people like that in it.

Result:

F.P. Crowder	Conservative	23 480
J.L. King	Labour	10 424
R.A. Walker	Liberal	7 295

Conservative majority 13 056

MY FIRST PARLIAMENTARY BY-ELECTION: HARROW WEST 17 MARCH 1960

Sir Albert Braithwaite, Tory MP for Harrow West, was pressed by his local Association to defend the seat at the 1959 general election as, having only just scraped home in 1955 *(majority: 17,297)* it was obvious that no one else could possibly hold it. Despite his misgivings he allowed himself to be persuaded and duly won, and the Association's fears of a reduced majority proved less than well-founded – it was now a wafer-thin 18,000. Two days later he shot himself. John Wallbridge was adopted as Liberal candidate for the ensuing by-election. Imagination and plagiarism combined to select our campaign slogan: 'Win With Wallbridge!'.

What I remember most clearly from that by-election – indeed, I remember little else – is that the Labour candidate, name of Jenkins, published an election address which clearly stated in bold capitals right across the bottom of the centrefold:

REMEMBER: LABOUR IS THE **ONLY** ALTERNATIVE TO THE TORIES

Technically untrue as this was as there were three non-Conservative candidates, not just one, you get the idea. It wasn't a new tactic then and even today all parties use this line when it suits them. The risk is that if it doesn't work you end up covered in egg (or, as one of my friends once inelegantly phrased it: 'Up to your arse in alligators').

In the election the previous year Jenkins had polled 12,512 in a straight fight, against Sir Albert's 30,512. The appearance of a Liberal candidate and Jenkins' pathological fear of the possible consequences informed his entire campaign, and he took every opportunity to proclaim to the electors that if they wanted to beat the Tories – their majority of 18,000 notwithstanding – then you could *only* do it by voting Labour. Sound familiar? The fact was that with a Tory majority that size *no one* was going to beat them, not even Jenkins if he got the entire Liberal and Independent vote to add to his own. He dismissed the Liberals as effete amateurs with no experience who knew nothing about politics and members of a party which had no policy. At the count I had the immense satisfaction of seeing his face when to his indescribable chagrin the despised and vilified Liberal beat him into third place. The ignominy – coming third behind what he had spent his entire campaign telling the public were a ragtag bag of losers, mis-fits and all the rest of it! To us, it was a welcome affirmation that as a party we were still in business, even if only to the extent of taking second place in a rock-solid Tory seat. But any second place is better than any third – and in the early sixties even second places were like manna from heaven. In private it was also, needless to say, a relief.

Result:

A.J. Page	Conservative	18 526
J. Wallbridge	Liberal	7 100
P.J. Jenkins	Labour	6 030
J.E. Dayton	Independent	1 560

Conservative majority 11 426

Anecdote No 6
Canvassing a terrace of 1930s-style houses, I knocked on one nondescript door and was somewhat discombobulated when it opened and as I looked straight ahead, as one does, there was no one there. Glancing down, the man of the house was looking me straight in the navel – not just because he was short of stature but also because his hallway was about a foot below the level of the doorstep.

He was dark-haired, middle-aged, wearing a multicoloured sleeveless pullover full of holes and tucked into his trousers, and clearly wearing neither shoes nor slippers as most of his toes were sticking out of his socks. Behind him up the hallway as far as the eye could see the carpet, similarly full of holes, was covered with bits of fluff, scraps of paper and assorted debris.

'I'm from the Liberals', I mumbled, recovering my composure.

He averted his gaze from my navel and looked me pleasantly in the eye.

'Nah. Tory, mate', he said, and closed the door.

My reaction to this episode was: he says he's a Conservative. What on earth has he got to conserve?

I've been puzzling this one ever since: the 'haves' will always naturally vote Conservative (unless they have an education, a conscience or preferably both). But why do lots of 'have nots' vote for them, too?

THE CARSHALTON BY-ELECTION: 16 NOVEMBER 1960

I don't remember the circumstances which necessitated the by-election, even less anything about the candidates, merely that by now THOR's fame was spreading and when by-elections occurred specialists such as us trained in polling day organisation were in demand.

I arrived on schedule at the station. I was met, by a total stranger. 'Are you the THOR expert?' 'Yes'. 'Get in.' I was driven to the committee room. I had no idea where it was, and never found out. I didn't need to know, as THOR techniques were standardised and could be slotted in and applied anywhere – a bit like plugging in your electric shaver in any hotel room in any foreign country, no matter where it is. The local volunteers working the area served by my committee room regarded me with the awe approximately appropriate to that due to an extra-terrestrial. Everything in the room was laid out *per* John Wallbridge's template as to what equipment was necessary, even down to the recommended number of pencils (already sharpened, of course), rubbers, bottles of glue (the brand *Gloy* was favoured), rulers, knocking-up sheets, etc. I stayed in the room all day, was fed and watered at regular intervals, and when the polls closed at nine o'clock thanked warmly for my services and taken back to the station and put on to my train home.

Result:

Capt. W.E. Elliott	Conservative	19 175
J.H.G. Browne	Liberal	10 250
B. Thomas	Labour	7 696

Conservative majority 8 925

I never saw anything of Carshalton itself, and only met the candidate and agent I was working for when they popped in on their rounds of all the committee rooms to say hello and thank you for coming.

That, of course, was the point. Because of our thorough THOR training, we could go to any by-election in any area whether we were familiar with it or not, and use the procedures and techniques we'd learned regardless of local circumstances – provided the locals had prepared the ground in accordance with THOR guidelines when writing up the results of canvassing, drawing up lists of tellers, knockers-up and so on. A constituency prepared to adopt THOR principles could, when a by-election occurred, invite totally unknown 'THOR experts' to be parachuted in and leave them to take charge and get on with it. Provided the locals had prepared the ground as laid down in THOR information sheets and manuals, we could.

In due course, the Party hierarchy recognised the value of the skills THOR taught its trainees and the importance of the standardised organisational methods it promoted in pursuit of electoral victory. Professionalism and method gradually replaced amateurism and wishful thinking – 'It'll all work out alright on the night' (*Oh! no it won't!*). Thanks to John's pioneering work with THOR, the Association of Liberal Councillors (ALC) saw the light of day, and when the party changed its name its successor, ALDC.

The party's debt of gratitude to John Wallbridge for thinking up THOR sadly was never acknowledged, let alone rewarded by formal recognition or an honour of some kind. It's too late now. He died in 1992.

BACK IN SOUTHAMPTON

At Easter in 1960 Margaret and I got married, and feathered our first marital love-nest (as opposed to the other sort we'd been enjoying for months) renting the upstairs in a three-bedroomed semi in Burgess Road, backing onto Southampton Common. As one wag put it: 'You newly-weds can watch the squirrels cavorting about, and they can do the same.' I'm not quite sure what he meant. A few months later we found ourselves expecting our first child, so went for broke (literally!) buying a semi of our own in Granby Grove, in a residential area immediately behind the University. The political point of this is that I no longer lived near the city centre, so began to detach myself from St Luke's and start working in Portswood, the ward I now lived in.

JO BOWLS A MAIDEN OVER

The university by now had a Liberal Club. I had a part-time contract in the Science Faculty under the banner of 'Science Russian', to teach research scientists how to read printed Cyrillic script well enough to be able to read the summaries of papers and periodicals published in Russian and get the gist well enough to be able to decide if they needed them to be fully translated. On this rather semi-detached basis, I had a loose connection to the student Liberal Club as technically a member of staff.

Anecdote No 7
The Liberal Club invited the party Leader, Jo Grimond, to come and address them, and he accepted. Afterwards, it fell to Margaret and I to entertain him to tea, so we took him to the Dolphin Hotel, an imposing Georgian building in down-town Southampton which, as it happens, had been our chosen venue for our wedding reception. Margaret was very impressed with how unassuming

and what generally good company Jo was, and when we'd put him safely on his train remarked, 'What a nice man!'

I think meeting Jo and being so favourably impressed helped her to make a decision which, in the light of her subsequent career in the party and in public life, was crucial. Initially she'd joined simply because I was involved. Henceforth, she became a Liberal activist in her own right. Jo could never have realised what a fire he unwittingly lit while we exchanged pleasantries over the teacups in the Dolphin lounge that day, and what immense consequences it would have on the local political landscape in Eastleigh a decade or so later – and for three decades thereafter .

SOUTHAMPTON CITY COUNCIL: PORTSWOOD WARD MAY 1961

There had been no Liberal candidate in Portswood in 1960, but later that year the branch, of which as a local resident I was now a member, adopted as Liberal candidate Peter Leigh, a self-employed cabinet maker who was unmarried and lived with his mother and other family members. We did the usual one-leaflet campaign and some canvassing – but then at the count the earth moved. I noticed that one of the polling staff who was counting the votes had put a ballot paper marked with a vote for Labour on top of a bundle of Liberal votes, and drew her attention to the error. This had the effect of knocking 99 votes off Labour's erstwhile total and adding them to ours:

Result:

J. Barr	Con-RP	2 082
P.D. Leigh	Liberal	659
Mrs Mills	Labour	591

Conservative majority 1 423

Finding that she'd come third behind the despised Liberal, the Labour candidate went absolutely ballistic – to use an expression *not* in current use at the time. In front of the assembled throng of

SOUTHAMPTON MUNICIPAL ELECTIONS
THURSDAY, 11th MAY, 1961

Mr. Peter LEIGH

*

Cabinet maker

Aged 25. Has lived most of his life in Portswood. Is a founder-member of Southampton Young Liberal Association.

51, Shaftesbury Avenue,
Highfield.
Tel. : 55875.

Ladies and Gentlemen,

For many years past we in Portswood Ward have not had the opportunity to vote for a Liberal candidate. This is an unfortunate state of affairs, and I know when faced with the choice of only two candidates many people with liberal sympathies have felt bound to vote for a party they disliked in order to keep out the other party which they disliked even more. This has resulted in people voting *against* candidates instead of *for* them.

As your Liberal candidate, I appeal for your support if you are a person who thinks of themselves as being liberal-minded. If you support me but do not *vote for* me, then you are wasting your vote. If you are a Liberal—then *VOTE* Liberal!

If elected as your Liberal councillor, I shall do my best to serve you along the lines indicated in my policy points on the opposite page. On the vexed question of the proposed extensions to the University, I stand four-square behind the Highfield Residents' Association. I am in favour of the University expanding, but not into people's homes when there are other sites available. As a Liberal I believe in the freedom of the individual, and so I am against compulsory purchase except in cases of absolute necessity, and provided that the people dispossessed are satisfactorily rehoused.

Finally, a vote for a Liberal councillor in Portswood is a first step towards achieving a Liberal Government in Westminster. Please remember this on Thursday, May 11th.

Yours sincerely,

PETER LEIGH.

FIVE POINTS

COMPULSORY PURCHASE

IS a political issue. Only Liberals put people's happiness before planners' convenience

RATES CAN BE CUT

by taxing the plot of land and not the buildings on it. In this way people who improve their houses would not have to pay extra rates.

YOUR CHILDREN

cannot get a good twentieth-century education in bad nineteenth-century school buildings. Nor are Army nissen huts a permanent substitute for proper classrooms.

WE DEPLORE

" party politics " in local affairs. A councillor should serve the people, not the party bosses.

★ ★ ★ ★ ★

WE WANT

Liberal councillors and eventually a Liberal M.P. to work for bigger old age pensions, better roads, schools and hospitals, lower taxes, a stronger United Nations and the scrapping of the British H-bomb.

LEIGH

LIBERAL

Published by M A R T I N K Y R L E, 14 Granby Grove, Highfield, Southampton and Printed by G. F. Wilson & Co. Ltd., Southampton.

candidates, agents and counting agents and the Returning Officer as he prepared to make the declaration, she accused me of electoral fraud because I'd 'stolen their vote'. Funny sort of logic, that. The 99 Liberal votes when inadvertently topped by one Labour one, by some variant of osmosis thereby became Labour votes. I am still waiting for someone to explain this thought process to me.

The importance of this result is that it was the first time since before the War that a Liberal had come second – it was, therefore, our first *second place* in living memory and a milestone of immense significance. In elections in Southampton the Liberals always but always came a very distant third – until now, at this count. Adding to Mrs Mills' disbelief and feelings of outrage at being beaten by a Liberal was the fact that she was the first Labour candidate it had happened to, and she knew she'd never live it down for the rest of her political life.

The following year Leigh held second place, and this time two other Liberals came second – one with a substantial four-figure vote in Millbrook, just ahead of Labour. Unfortunately the Association itself was on the point of imploding due to personal animosities, and in the years immediately following – by which time I'd moved house and was no longer living in Southampton – the Liberals reverted to third place.

SOUTHAMPTON CITY COUNCIL: THE ALDERMANIC BY-ELECTIONS, 29 JUNE 1961

The Tories, in Southampton in those days called Conservative and Ratepayer, did well in the council elections in May 1961 and were able to augment their presence in the council chamber by nominating four of their councillors as aldermen (who were elected by fellow-councillors, not by the public). On election as an alderman, a councillor resigned his seat and a by-election was held – for which reason parties didn't normally put a councillor forward for the aldermanic bench unless his ward was safe and they could depend on holding it in the ensuing by-election. The nomination of two councillors from the same ward, Shirley, created a double vacancy there.

We had no party members in the area able or willing to stand, so had to find two outsiders. One was Arthur Pratt, 40-ish going on 20, rode a large motorbike and liked to turn up to meetings in his leathers to make an impression (which he did, but maybe not the one he thought he was making). Margaret had begun complaining about the number of evenings I was out at Liberal meetings, leaving her at home with the baby, so I told her, 'If you can't beat 'em, join 'em'. Why don't you stand as the other Liberal candidate and *I'll* stay home and baby-sit?' She took me up on my offer.

When nominations closed the line-up was most peculiar: albeit all three wards were rock-solid Tory, Labour were the only other party on the city council yet they were fielding a candidate in only one ward. In Portswood our previous candidate Peter Leigh was given a straight fight. In Shirley the nominations for the double vacancy were two Conservatives, two Liberals and two

34

Communists. The Communist Party, so we were told, only put up candidates for council elections if there was a minimum of 25 paid-up party members in the ward, to guarantee any Communist standing for election at least 25 votes. And one of their two candidates did, indeed, get just that number. But not the other. The plot thickens.

Liberal candidate Margaret Kyrle in 1961 (aged 23)

This being a by-election to fill two vacancies, voters going to the polls had two votes. By chance, the first two names on the ballot paper were the two Conservatives, Barnes and Dawson. The next name was Gibbs, one of the Communists, then Kyrle and Pratt and finally the second Commie, Shannon.

Seeing that the two names at the top of the paper were both Tories, it seems some people assumed from this that the candidates were paired in political party order: if the first pair were the Conservatives, it followed that the next pair were also of the same party, and as the first of these was Gibbs the Communist the next name, Kyrle, must be the other one. Nowadays, as we all know, candidates are allowed to show their party affiliations – if any – in their personal descriptions on ballot papers, but back then such information was forbidden by electoral law – hence the confusion.

It therefore appears that some of those voting Communist for Gibbs then cast their second vote for the next name on the ballot paper – Kyrle – because they thought that she was the second Communist. If this prognostication is true, then in addition to all the genuine Liberal votes for Kyrle and Pratt, Kyrle also got a bonus of misplaced Communist votes intended for the second Communist candidate, who unfortunately for alphabetical reasons was the last name on the list. To cut a long story short, Margaret Kyrle ended up with more votes than Arthur Pratt.

Result:

G.C. Barnes	Con-RP	1 754
J.J. Dawson	Con-RP	1 717
Mrs M.R.Kyrle	Liberal	376
A.L. Pratt	Liberal	325
T.G. Gibbs	Communist	63
R. Shannon	Communist	25

Conservative majority (average) 1 385

The balloon went up – and A. Pratt lived down to his name and behaved like one. Presumably on the basis that he was (a) a man, and (b) twice Margaret's age, he saw himself as the 'senior' Liberal candidate and this slip of a girl getting fifty more votes than him was a direct and public insult. He demanded that she should apologise and resign. If she didn't, *he* would. She didn't, and he did.

You may be utterly amazed that a candidate could be so petty and childish over the matter of coming a few votes behind a party colleague in a multiple election. On the other hand, you may not – I regret to say that when *vintage A. Pratt '61* blew his top (or was it his cork?) that wasn't the final squeezing of that particular choice fruit – many of us will have come across the *prima donna* tendency in other circumstances. But on this occasion there were absolutely no grounds for Pratt's complaints. Margaret had not done anything to get those extra votes. Names on ballot papers are in alphabetical order, and she just happened to have a surname beginning with a letter which came before his – hardly something to apologise for, far less tender her resignation from the party. The discrepancy in the number of votes received was partly explicable by confusion amongst Communist supporters misreading the ballot paper, partly by the element of cross-voting which always takes place in multiple elections and partly by people just casting one vote, for the first Liberal, and not voting for the second Liberal because they forgot they had two votes – something which always happens in multiple elections. Superficially, the discrepancy between the votes of the two Communists candidates shows more than twice as many electors were willing to vote for Gibbs than would vote for Shannon, but why should they give their second vote to a Liberal – politically the polar opposite? It's pretty obvious what really happened – they made a mistake. When these possibilities were explained to Pratt it made not a blind bit of difference. He remained adamant that he'd been insulted, and if the Association didn't back him and secure an apology from the other candidate he was finished with the Liberal Party.

Further little local difficulties: the Association having no money to fight the elections, it had been agreed that the two candidates would share the cost equally between them – £9, for a one-leaflet campaign. To a modern eye so small a sum probably looks like small change or at the very least a misprint – you've left a nought off. But by way of comparison look, for example, at my salary then as a new teacher with what the Ministry of Education officially classified as a 'good degree' (the starting salary for graduates with a First or Upper Second was £720pa instead of £520pa). In round figures, it was £15 a week. Margaret and I had been prepared to stump up her half – £4.10s 0d. – even though it was something like two days' pay and a considerable sacrifice for a young couple with a baby and a mortgage and trying to furnish a house, living off one salary. As Agent, I was responsible for paying the election expenses. As Pratt had waltzed away from his obligations consumed with indignation and accusing Margaret of personally insulting him, he was obviously not going to honour his side of the bargain.

The only way out was to pay the expenses within the legal time limit and then do some fund-raising to recoup my outlay. I arranged a jumble sale, made £4.10s.0d profit – which conveniently covered what Pratt should have contributed – and paid it into my bank account to ensure I didn't go overdrawn. All square. Thanks to a personal contribution coupled with profits from a fundraising event, by-election expenses all paid without asking the Association for a penny.

We never saw Pratt again.

THE ORPINGTON BY-ELECTION: 14 MARCH 1962

Because it took place on a day when I wasn't teaching, I was able to get to Orpington to knock-up. I never saw, let alone met, Eric Lubbock, but I still have my copy of his election address – and very staid and dated it looks compared to modern styles. On the way back home to Southampton, in the middle of nowhere and at about two in the morning, my car broke down. It was a 1936 Morris 8 cobbled together by a student friend from two vehicles we'd bought at a car auction for £10 the pair and then cannibalised, returning at the next auction to sell some of the duplicated parts and recouping about a quarter of our original outlay. Fortunately, I had three engineering students from the university who'd hitched a lift to come and knock up with me, and they had the required skills to effect running repairs. One of them found a telephone box to phone home to explain our non-arrival back at the expected time and assure everyone that we had not been involved in a traffic accident. At home, they'd heard the declaration of the result and so, marooned by the roadside, God-knows-where in the wee small hours and with car parts all around us lit by torchlight, we heard that we'd won the by-election with a majority of 7,855. It had

ORPINGTON PARLIAMENTARY BY-ELECTION

POLLING DAY: WEDNESDAY, 14th MARCH

POLLING 7·0 a.m. — 9·0 p.m.

LIBERAL CENTRAL COMMITTEE ROOMS

are at

CARLTON CINEMA, CARLTON PARADE ORPINGTON

Telephone: Orpington 22761

PRINTED BY
CHAS. F. THORN & SON LTD. (T.U.), 58-64 WELLINGTON STREET, WOOLWICH, S.E.18
PUBLISHED BY
P. CHITNIS, AGENT, CARLTON CINEMA, CARLTON PARADE, ORPINGTON, KENT

after all been worth our time, money and effort to drive the best part of 200 miles to drag in those extra voters, break-down or no break-down.

If ever I do meet Lord Avebury, it's still not too late to thank me.

SOUTHAMPTON CITY COUNCIL: ST LUKE'S, 1963

George Payne had decided to retire from the fight, and there was no Liberal candidate in St Luke's ward in the 1962 elections. Peter Leigh had stood again in Portswood, and held on to second place. I'd fallen out with his mother, who had revealed her true political attitudes by regaling us all one evening over coffee after a committee meeting about which parts of the private anatomy of sex offenders she would like to take a sharp instrument to, in such descriptive detail that had Torquemada himself been listening I imagine he would have been surreptitiously checking the presence and number of his genitalia. She didn't sound much like a Liberal to me, and when Peter sided with her that was the end of it so far as I was concerned. Soon after that he resigned from the party, and his replacement as candidate in Portswood in 1963 came third.

Due to the unpleasant atmosphere in Portswood, I decided instead to be Agent in St Luke's, with Margaret as our candidate (*v supra about having a committee room with a window straight onto the pavement outside, and letting no one in*).

Result:

E.W. Clark	Labour	1 378
J.R.H. Adams	Con-RP	1 171
Mrs M.R. Kyrle	Liberal	559
J.P. Bonnin	Communist	64

Labour gain. Majority 207

Anecdote No 8
Margaret went canvassing alone one evening in down-town St Luke's, and when she came back remarked on how surprised she'd been at finding so many young women and most of them living alone. 'But they were all very nice to me', she said.

We hadn't told her that this was the 'red light' district! When she found out she put two and two together and worked it out that they'd all been so nice to her because they didn't see her as competition! She was 24, very pretty, endowed by nature with an ample figure (and knew it, and who would I be to argue?) – and felt thoroughly insulted!

One serious observation. Back then in 1963 we felt perfectly confident that if we sent a 24-year old girl out in the evening, canvassing the 'red light' district alone, she would come to no harm (and we were right – she didn't). Would we do that in that part of Southampton – or indeed any similar-sized town – nowadays?

Anecdote No 9
Nothing to do with politics, but on the subject of Margaret feeling insulted I must tell you this one.

When our first child was born new mum insisted on buying a Silver Cross pram, even though it cost nearly a fortnight's wages. It was a huge sit-up-and-beg beast, and as Margaret was only 5ft 3½ins she was almost dwarfed by it when out pushing baby and with the hood up.

She decided one afternoon to meet me from school, proudly pushing said enormous pram. As she came into the playground, one of the boys saw her, leaned out of the window and shouted, 'Ey look! It's Old Ma Kyrle wiv' a kid!'

What really mortified her was the 'old'. 'What's he mean', she protested. 'Old Ma Kyrle? I'm 24, for God's sake!'

Shows how kids judge age, doesn't it.

Relations within the Association continued to deteriorate, from fraught to dire. We had acquired a new chairman, E.J. Bradbury, a self-opinionated, overbearing individual who'd devised some crack-brained scheme to do with taxation and hawked it round all three political parties in turn. The Tories and Labour had told him where to stick it, but the Liberals had been a bit more polite and fobbed him off with 'We'll take a look', which he misread as support for his ideas and on the strength of that misunderstanding joined the party. But he was not a Liberal in any sense of the word, being both temperamentally and in terms of his real political beliefs a right-wing Tory of the blustering 'Colonel Blimp' type. I always regarded him as a snake-oil salesman in a suit because he'd served in the RAF in the War but would never tell us what rank he'd held – merely assuring us that it was 'something pretty decent', whatever that was supposed to mean. Simply because I was half his age he expected me to treat his every pronouncement with fawning respect, and there was no love lost between us when he found it wasn't forthcoming and that I didn't respect him as much as he did (it would hardly have been possible – it would have used up the world's entire reserves). I also suspected that he resented the fact that I'd been an officer in the navy during national service. Decoded, 'something pretty decent' was glaringly obviously not commissioned rank, because Bradbury was the sort of man who would have had it monogrammed on his jock strap let alone used it in front of his name on a business card (we've all met 'em). All this combined to reinforce his determination to get rid of me as a dangerous subversive if he could manipulate an excuse.

Hitherto all regular Liberal activity in Southampton had been confined to the Test constituency, but for some time as Agent I had been seeking ways to develop Liberal activity across the river in the city's other parliamentary seat, Southampton Itchen. In the course of visiting potential recruits I met Jo Cherryson, who lived with his parents in a flat in Woolston and who I signed up as a party member while he was sitting in my car debating with me at about two in the morning. They had arrived from Poland as refugees with their children, and had changed their name from Wisniewski to the approximate English translation, Cherryson. At the time of his arrival Jo was about 15, and although he'd learned to speak perfect English unfortunately it was with a heavy Polish accent – a fate his siblings, arriving at a younger age, managed to avoid. He'd been to university, which was not so common in those days and showed how successfully he'd integrated himself into his adopted country.

We became great friends, and Margaret and I later attended his wedding at the Catholic Church of the Immaculate Conception near the bottom of the road where we lived.

Bradbury moved forward with his plans to get me off the Executive by starting to hold meetings at times when I couldn't attend, even though I was still officially the election agent for every ward and needed to be kept in the picture. I knew perfectly well what was afoot, because the treasurer, David Trotman, was a firm friend who – understanding the vital importance of the work I did day in and day out as Agent, trying to promote efficient methods of fighting elections – acted as my eyes and ears. Jo and I laid plans for our next move if and when Bradbury finally brought matters to a head and did something irreversible. David told me when Bradbury and his clique finally settled for a final throw of the dice: a motion to go before the next Executive meeting to expel me from the party 'because of all the harm I was doing'. They didn't specify anything particularly damning, a sure indication that they didn't have anything to hold against me that would bear serious independent examination. They complained rather vaguely about some of my letters in the local press, which inevitably (and often intentionally) drew responses from the opposition and provoked arguments. But writing to the press either defending your party's policies or attacking those of other parties has always been a perfectly legitimate political activity. Bradbury informed me that I was not invited to this Executive meeting and could not attend (no case here of the accused being allowed to defend himself – real liberalism, Bradbury-style, that was!), and threatened that if I ignored his warning and showed up he would personally throw me down the stairs. David, who was about fifteen stone and of stocky build, told me to take no notice and turn up. I was, after all, a *member* of the Executive, so perfectly entitled to attend any of its meetings whether the chairman liked it or not. If things really did descend to physical violence, he assured me that he would physically protect me and sort Bradbury out.

It didn't come to that. I turned up for the meeting, was told it was private and the door was shut in my face. That was the signal for Jo and I to fire-up Plan A. He was, as arranged, waiting for me outside in his car. We went off to his house and rolled out the plans we had prepared for the inaugural meeting of Southampton *Itchen* Liberal Association as a separate Association from Southampton Test, which Bradbury and his sycophants had control of. Three weeks later, at a meeting to which all paid-up party members in the Itchen constituency were invited, Southampton Itchen Liberal Association was formally established. Six weeks later, Southampton Test Liberal Association imploded.

I rest my case.

[NB It's interesting to note that in those days a local Association had the power to expel a member not merely from the Association but from the party itself. Such power was open to serious misuse, and one wonders how many potentially valuable members across the country the party lost because of the malign influence of local cliques able to manipulate the rules and keep out anyone whose face didn't fit.]

Anecdote No 10
Jo Cherryson was Liberal candidate for Southampton Itchen at the 1964 general election. His method of using a loudspeaker van largely explains, at least to me, why we no longer use this device.

He would start his speech at the beginning of a road, continue speaking uninterrupted along its length, and time it to finish at the end of the road. He never worked out for himself the reason why this tactic doesn't work, namely that those who hear the first part of the speech don't hear the conclusion – possibly the punch-line or the reason why everyone listening should vote Liberal – while at the same time those who hear the punch-line at the end haven't heard the first part so don't know what the speaker's talking about. In Jo's case, moreover, the whole was delivered in a thick Polish accent which was often difficult to understand for people who weren't used to it and totally unintelligible when coming over a loudspeaker from a vehicle in motion. Effective as a way of campaigning? Not. But Jo never understood this. Bless!

He was always frightfully upbeat about how well his campaign was going, and everyone likes the candidate to be positive and reassuring and exude confidence. But there are limits. When you're the first Liberal to contest the constituency for almost twenty years and your primary objective is to save your deposit, it is actually rather destabilising if not dispiriting for party workers to be constantly regaled by the candidate with over-estimates of public support and musings about how large his majority is likely to be.

To describe Jo I coined the phrase 'a depressing optimist'.

SOUTHAMPTON IN THE GENERAL ELECTION OF 1964

ITCHEN

H.M. King	Labour	28 949
G.G. Olson	Conservative	18 974
J. Cherryson	Liberal	7 007

Labour majority 9 975

TEST

Sir J. Fletcher-Cooke	Conservative	25 700
R.C. Mitchell	Labour	25 352

Conservative majority 348

Anecdote No 11
Group Captain Fulljames was much revered as a sort of 'elder statesman', partly because he'd been our candidate donkey's years ago (1945, directly after the War, in fact – in another world!) and possibly also because there weren't that many ex-service officers of his senior rank who were Liberal supporters. He lived in a large country house out at Curdridge, but retained an honorary position in Southampton as, I think, President.

On one occasion he was addressing a public meeting in support of our candidate and was asked a rather tricky question by an elderly lady in the audience. He gave a somewhat rambling, equivocal reply – basically, he was treading water (I was present, by the way – this isn't hearsay). He finished by saying to the questioner, 'And I'm with you on that question'. 'Yes', she shot back, 'and you haven't answered it'.

One nil, I think.

In the summer of 1963 I'd been offered a part-time contract at Winchester County High School for Girls to introduce Russian into the curriculum, with a promise of a permanent full-time post when I'd got the first batch of pupils through O level and with an A level class to follow could sustain a full timetable. I made up the shortfall by teaching a bit of history and, as a new venture, took the Lower Sixth for a course in PPE – politics, philosophy, ethics and elementary logic, where by way of introduction to the course I explained to the girls, 'I'm not here to teach you *what* to think, but *how* to think. And I must warn you – thinking for yourself can be dangerous. You may start with a point of view, think it through and end up disagreeing with yourself. Or your friends. Or your parents. There can be repercussions, and a price to pay.' Back to the point: in the summer of 1965 that promise was honoured. Margaret and I decided that this was the opportune moment to up sticks and move, and in doing so we severed all connection with politics in Southampton and with Southampton Liberal Party.

We wanted a house with a large garden where the children could play, and I could embed myself in the practices of my rural childhood: growing my own fruit and veg and keeping chickens. *(Margaret: 'Keeping chickens? Over my dead body!' Me: 'That can be arranged.')* We couldn't afford a house in Winchester – how times have changed (*not!*) – so cutting our coat according to our cloth, although we did manage to move 'up north' it was only as far as Chandler's Ford. This was in a different constituency – Eastleigh

– where our local torch-bearer and parliamentary candidate was an old friend – John Foster Rice. The day after we moved in, I rang John at his home in Lower Upham and said, 'John, I've moved into your constituency. Find me a candidate, and I'll fight the next elections for you in Chandler's Ford'. He did, and in 1966 I was Agent once again. But that's another story, to be unravelled to general delight and occasional horror in Part 2.

EPILOGUE

When Chris Huhne MP pressed me to put this personal History down on paper it was, perhaps, partly in recognition of the fact that, simply due to *anno domini*, I am one of the few surviving eye-witnesses involved in Southampton Liberal Party in the middle of the last century – indeed, possibly the last. I am certainly the only one still alive who has remained continuously active in the party and still heavily involved on a daily basis *(as I write, bundles of the latest Focus lie on the table behind me for delivery – there these 24 hours!)*. But I warned him, 'You'll need to be sitting down when you read some of the tales that'll be in it. You won't believe that such richly grotesque people who 'ran' the Liberal Party in those days could possibly be real, and you'll fall over laughing from uncontrollable incredulity and do yourself a mischief!'. I think Chris wanted a serious academic monograph. I'm afraid that isn't what I've written, and I'm sorry if I've disappointed him.

But, insofar as my memory for minor details serves me correctly, everything recounted here did take place and I stand by my judgments. The berks who ponced around calling themselves Liberals and purporting to be running a political party really did have no idea how to do it, and in general really were determined not to learn. With a few honourable and very admirable exceptions, their attitude was 'We've always done it like this.' 'Does it work?' 'No. But we've always done it like this.' Full stop. End of story. As was posited earlier on: they kept the party alive, but at the same time they killed it.

To understand why this situation was the case, consider the straits the Liberal Party was in nationally in the late 1950s/early 1960s. Liberal MPs in the House of Commons could usually be counted on the fingers of one hand, and two of them, in Bolton West and Huddersfield West, were only there because of local 'arrangements' with the Conservatives to give them a straight fight with Labour in return, *quid pro quo*, for us giving them an equally contrived free run in the other seat. In general elections, the result for most of our candidates was third place and miles behind and a lost deposit of a hundred and fifty quid to rub your nose in it. *[Question: in a democracy, offering oneself for election is surely every man's (and woman's) right. So why should you have to put down a substantial cash deposit in order to exercise a right? If it's a right, why should one be asked to pay for it? Or is democracy only for the rich, and for the poor – tough?]*. With little chance of getting elected and no possibility of an influential and therefore meaningful political career, why would anyone with talent or ambition join a party membership of which – especially active, i.e. public, membership – brought as an additional cross to bear general ridicule from the press and public, let alone one's political opponents?

If people with talent, ability and ambition declined as a general rule to join the Liberals, who does that leave? Answer: those *without* talent, ability or ambition, along with those seeking to be very large frogs in very small ponds. To this lack of suitability for the job was often allied inordinate conceit coupled with a marked absence of the three senses: of humour, of proportion and common. This predicament damaged the party in two ways. On the one hand, local associations were being run by people with no understanding of how to do it properly, while at the same time people with more ability were put off from joining by the prospect of having to work with or even sit round a committee table with party officers who were clearly incapable and into the bargain often excessively touchy and self-regarding.

There was hardly any national organisation. For lack of funds to permit any greater provision by way of professional staff, the whole of the Home Counties was managed from an office in Victoria St. in London by a single official, Diana Stephenson. I got to know her quite well over several years and admired immensely her practical, down-to-earth common sense in dealing with some highly volatile party members. No training was offered for aspiring MPs or constituency officers, most of whom, in my experience, didn't think they *needed* any training – the more inept they were, the more tenaciously they defended their ineptitude and their right to be so. To some of them, bumbling chaos was a badge to be worn with pride – proof that they were genuine Liberals – and becoming efficient was viewed as highly suspect – were you *really* a Liberal? Learn from my mistakes? *What* mistakes? They would have been affronted had someone suggested that they might go on a training course or attend a workshop – which partly explains why no such things existed until many years later when the national party started to get professional. Elected councillors, of whom, *mirabile dictu*, there were one or two scattered about, were left to fend for themselves, should they, by some extraordinary throw of the dice, buck the norm and win a seat.

The modern party contains many older members who have valuable experience and can give sound advice *(been there, done that, etc.)* That, too, is a major difference between then and now. There were 'older members', of course. But they had never won an election, had never bothered to work out why not and much as some of them loved to give advice it was absolutely worthless. The modern party is chock-full of experienced councillors, experienced former councillors, people who are or have been chairmen of committees or governing bodies, mayor of their town or city or chairman of their local authority and all the rest of it, or have years of experience and know-how as successful agents, fund-raisers, conference or polling day organisers and practical experience in writing leaflets, election materials and the ubiquitous *Focus*. Around the country there are hundreds of members who, like me, have in the past at various times fulfilled all of these roles in the service of the party and the public. Activists fifty years ago had no one to turn to for help or sensible advice, and no successful role models to look to for inspiration.

Another sea-change in the past fifty years is the attitude of the other parties. There may be a bit of pushing and shoving, but Liberal Democrat campaigners and candidates nowadays are treated by other parties' activists with the same level of mutual respect as they treat each other. However much our opponents may disagree with us, they don't question our right to exist as such (much as they may say otherwise in private!). Our position as a credible party is accepted, as are our claims to have our policies taken seriously and subjected to proper examination and our record in office assessed. (NB this last is because in many areas we *have* a record in office to be assessed, which was not the case then).

The almost tangible arrogance of the other parties in their attitude towards the Liberals was something the modern generation can scarcely begin to imagine. Putting up a Liberal candidate in an election was regarded by Labour and the Tories as a preposterous intrusion, and indeed they regularly accused us – and I quote – of 'intervening' if we put someone up in an election. The subliminal accusation was, 'Don't you people understand that elections are between our two parties, and we are the only ones entitled to stand?'. It was standard practice, particularly amongst Labour candidates, to declaim to the public in a rather lofty and disdainful manner that 'the Liberals have NO POLICY' (always in capital letters). If you fell for it and sent them a booklet from HQ they'd then come back saying they'd read it, and like they'd said – we had no policy. Ha! ha!, bloody ha! It was as childish as that, with sarcasm reigning supreme. The truth is, Tories and Labour in those days regarded Liberals rather as whites in the days of segregation in the former Confederate States regarded what in their circles they called 'uppity niggers': second class citizens, know your place and keep to it. Stand for election to the council? Who do you think you are? It's against this background that one should judge the reaction of the Labour candidate in Portswood Ward in 1961 when the Liberal beat her into third place – *lèse majesté* would be an apt comparison.

One brick the opposition regularly threw at us, though, was well founded: 'the Liberals have no experience'. It was true

– we hadn't had anyone on the council for a generation. They sometimes followed this up by asking what was the point of electing a Liberal when he or she would be the only one on the council facing a phalanx of opponents from the other two parties and in consequence completely without power or influence. Here again the difference between then and now is stark: no Tory or Labour candidate today would try this line of argument, because they'd be laughed at.

My riposte to such an accusation used to be 'Maybe our candidates haven't got experience, but they do have talent!' Everyone knows councillors who've sat on the council for years without ever learning – or perhaps bothering – to carry out their duties conscientiously, and no matter how many years they spend gaining 'experience' they're still dross. Their personal indolence or lack of basic *nous* makes them – let's be generous and say – 'light-weight' members of the local authority. And I blush to admit that there are Liberal Democrat councillors like that, too.

A FINAL QUESTION

Some readers may be wondering: if things were as ghastly as you tell us they were, why did you stick it out? Masochism, perhaps?

I like to think that it's because I joined the Liberal Party simply out of a philosophical belief in its principles, and considerations of career, wealth, public approval or position didn't come into it. There were, of course, others like me, even in those days, and some who joined and were far more successful than I was and carved out careers for themselves and became MPs or ended up in the House of Lords. Just not very many.

Anecdote No 12
I remember one afternoon – it must have been early in 1959 – running into the secretary of the University Labour Club on the steps of the West Building [NB – that was the Students' Union part]. *Somehow he'd heard about my recent decision to join the*

Liberals, and was anxious to seize this opportunity to patronise me for my unworldliness. We began to debate our respective parties' policies, and on every count my position was more left than his. 'You're not really a socialist', I said to him. 'You're just a careerist who wants a seat in Parliament'. He didn't demur, but responded by telling me dismissively, 'You're wasting your time in the Liberal Party. You'll never get anywhere.' 'Maybe,' I said, 'but at least I can sleep at nights.'

Seven years of working for the Liberals in Southampton produced no measurable political progress, bar that first time as runner-up in a council election and the blip of making it three the following year. The hours spent in committee meetings or delivering election addresses were, taken in the round, a waste of time. But how did the situation there compare with neighbouring constituencies? At the time, I had no idea. By the end of the '60s I'd discovered that some other Liberal Associations elsewhere in Hampshire paralleled Southampton. They, too, were in the hands of cliques who conspired together to keep control and exclude any new blood should some newcomer turn up keen to join the party and get stuck in working to increase membership and sharpen up campaigning strategy. That I made this discovery was due to the setting up of the first skeleton prototype of a county-wide party organisation – HALG, the Hampshire Area Liberal Group. A number of us wanted to create some sort of formal liaison body, even if low-key and low-budget, to link constituency associations and where appropriate to co-ordinate Liberal activity, e.g. get county council candidates from all parts to a seminar to debate and agree a policy platform for Hampshire County Council elections, instead of each constituency 'doing its own thing' in hermetically-sealed isolation. Later, as county chairman, together with the county secretary, Tony Hill, I had occasion to visit other Hampshire constituencies in an official capacity. What we found was sometimes absolutely unbelievable – and will be recounted in Part 2.

Most of my political experience in Southampton was of barely vestigial value, except getting hands-on experience of being a local election agent and thus able to bring to my new branch in Chandler's Ford a well-honed understanding of how to fight local elections using the practical skills promoted by THOR. Now, knowing what had to be done, negative experience in the quagmire of Southampton meant I knew how to achieve it, e.g. what sort of people to promote and work with and what other sort, because they would jeopardise any prospects of success, should be circumvented as a prelude to getting them dumped – no repetition of allowing silly old ladies to waste everybody's time arguing about entrance prices to jumble sales. Modern-day members and Local Party officers need to consider: it may be an Augean stable, but if you are seriously determined to make the party successful you cannot in the long run escape from the necessity of trying to clear it out – no matter how much metaphorical 'blood on the floor' you end up with (or, in keeping with the stable analogy, shit to get shot of).

In focussing attention after the passage of half a century on my seven year political apprenticeship in Southampton in order to write this very personal history, I have recalled to mind many half-forgotten events, some of them amusing at the time, others only in retrospect. Some episodes were distinctly unpleasant, and while it may be amusing or illuminating to read about those days of yore, happily it is unlikely that anyone joining the party nowadays would have to endure such ordeals. Some of the people one was forced into company with were themselves thoroughly unpleasant – but as we all know human nature remains fundamentally the same and doesn't change with the passage of time. We just deal with problems differently nowadays.

The Liberal Party in my young days accepted anyone who wanted to join, without questioning their reasons or their suitability for office, and incurred the inevitable outcomes. Fortunately, amongst those who joined the Liberals there were also a handful with genuine or almost superhuman talent who succeeded against the odds. Two such contemporary examples were Mark Bonham Carter, who won the Torrington by-election in 1958 (just before my time), and Jeremy Thorpe, who in Devon North in 1959 made our first gain in an English seat in a general election since pre-war days and went on to lead the party.

Despite its long and honourable history, the Liberal Party in the middle of the last century had become in many, perhaps most, areas such a shadow of its former self as to merit description as a 'fringe party', and attracted by and large the sort of people always found on the 'fringes'. But by the late '70s the party had started the long process of modernising itself and becoming more professional, raising serious money, employing more paid staff and in consequence winning more elections – particularly at local authority level. The existing members of the unreconstructable tendency were gradually sidelined or encouraged to leave of their own accord – to audible sighs of relief from the rest of us who were glad to be rid of them. They went off to found or find new 'fringe parties', where as bullfrogs in ponds of ever more manifest insignificance they could shout their mouths off championing this or that group of disaffected members of society who were determined to carry a banner or maintain an impossible demand even if they had to knit it themselves. One such example in modern times was the Natural Law Party, which was founded with much trumpeting in 1992 and whose 310 candidates at the general election received on average 0.19% of the vote. At the 1997 election they still managed to find the money to put up 197 candidates – who did even worse, averaging 0.10%. The NLP folded in 2003 and is only remembered, if at all, because those of us who saw them in a party political broadcast on TV bouncing about cross-legged on mattresses and calling it 'yogic flying' laughed so much we've never forgotten. There were and are other 'fringe' parties, with the sort of people in them that I am so *very* glad we no longer have in ours.

The political world in the middle of the twentieth century was in most essentials alien to ours in the second decade of the twenty-first. Judged overall, Southampton Liberal Party's officers in the early 1960s ballsed things up – I know because I was there, and indeed at times I was one of them *(OK – mea bloody culpa!)*. But putting derision to one side, ask yourself: could they, given their personal shortcomings and limitations allied to the absence of any advice or the exercise of any supervision let alone – dare one suggest it? – *authority* from such hierarchy as the party nationally had in place, have done much better with what they had – particularly with the people (the 'human resources') – at their disposal, and struggling against two firmly entrenched 'other parties' much more dominant then than they are now? There's probably a good MPhil thesis awaiting anyone who explores that question.

POSTSCRIPT:

Anecdote No 13
On 14 March 2012 the fund-raising Orpington Circle held a dinner at the National Liberal Club to mark the 50th anniversary of the eponymous by-election, with the winner, Eric Lubbock, subsequently Lord Avebury, as Guest of Honour and a host of party dignitaries, general well-wishers and veterans of that election in attendance . When I introduced myself to his Lordship as a humble foot soldier who'd helped out on the day but never received a word of thanks, he remarked 'I'll do that now', shook my hand and kindly autographed the copy of his election address which I'd brought along with me.

LIBERALISM   AND THE FAMILY

★ STOP WASTE ON DEFENCE

Britain spends £300m. a year on maintaining an independent nuclear deterrent, wastefully duplicating American efforts and obliging us to maintain expensive foreign bases. We should stop making the H-bomb and instead build up our conventional forces under NATO, as far as this can be done without endangering our balance of payments. Further, while realising that at present the West must retain the deterrent, we should work for general disarmament.

★ SIMPLIFY TAXATION

The cost of tax collection has trebled since the war, reaching £50m. in 1960. The tax system should be simplified to remove the many unnecessary complexities embodied in it. National Insurance and Graduated Pension contributions should be merged in a single Social Security tax, graded according to income; short term capital gains should be taxed; the surtax concessions should be deferred until they can be afforded; and wider property ownership should be encouraged through tax concessions.

★ ENTER THE COMMON MARKET

Britain must enter the Common Market. Important changes are already occurring in Europe which are speeding up technological progress there, while British industry remains insulated behind high tariff barriers.

Immediate steps should be taken towards a decimal currency system and the metric system of weights and measures, to help us compete in Europe on an equal footing.

★ . . . BUT SAFEGUARD THE COMMONWEALTH

Commonwealth countries must be kept fully informed of our Common Market negotiations. We should attempt to secure tariff-free quotas for certain Commonwealth products such as New Zealand butter and Australian beef.

★ STOP URBAN SPRAWL

London is choking to death. The programme for new and expanded towns must be accelerated and office building in already congested cities controlled. This would enable us to preserve the remaining open spaces in fringe areas such as Orpington, and relieve overcrowded trains and buses.

★ FOREIGN AFFAIRS

The U.N. can only work if it is fully representative; therefore, Red China has to be admitted. The division of Germany into two nations must be accepted and the Oder-Neisse boundary recognised. Berlin's freedom should be guaranteed by making it a U.N. controlled city.

★ PLAN AHEAD

Panic manipulations of Bank Rate and H.P. regulations, and the unco-ordinated scramble for higher wages are symptoms of a damaging failure to plan on a national scale, which any housewife would be ashamed of in her domestic budget.

Increases in dividends, as well as wages and salaries, should be regulated within a forecast rate of growth, giving full weight to the need for increased social and industrial investment. There must also be closer control of Government spending in the rationalized industries, and a reduction in the bill for subsidies.

★ . . . AND KEEP THE COST OF LIVING DOWN

Consumers should be represented on the National Economic Development Council, the Government's advisory group on planning. Everybody is a consumer, and agreements reached between employers and Trade Unions should not be at the expense of the general public. Retail price maintenance should be made illegal.

★ HELP OLD AGE PENSIONERS

The basic pension should be increased and tied to the cost of living index. The pernicious earnings rule should be abolished. Old people should not have to pay the 2/- prescription charge.

★ HEALTH MATTERS

Farnborough Hospital recently closed an operating theatre through staff shortages. The Government proposes to build many new hospitals, but unless immediate steps are taken to improve conditions of service, there will be no staff to man them.

★ SPEND MORE ON HOUSING

Despite long housing lists and acres of uncleared slums, public expenditure on housing has declined in recent years. There should be an increased housing budget as part of the Five-Year Plan, properly related to the capacity of the building industry. In this way fast growing Orpington's housing problem could be solved.

We must ensure, particularly, that the needs of the elderly are protected.

★ PRIORITY FOR EDUCATION

Britain spends less than half as much per head on education as the U.S. or Russia. The school building programme must be expanded and teachers' salaries raised. A greater number of talented young men and women would then be recruited into the profession, so that the size of classes could be reduced.

To ensure equality of opportunity, all education authorities should be required to provide the same facilities. Orpington has long needed a boys' grammar school and technical schools, and many primary schools need modernising.

Photo: Michael O'Sullivan

58

Liberal activists who travel many miles to give practical support to by-election candidates don't do so with any expectation of thanks, reimbursement of their costs or tangible reward, but go out of conviction and strength of party allegiance. They know perfectly well that they will, likely as not, be taken completely for granted and, as was my own experience at Orpington, it's highly unlikely that anyone will bother to thank them. Such treatment is accepted with a shrug of the shoulders and possibly a rueful acknowledgment that this is just the way things are, and no one complains because party loyalists with this level of commitment are tough cookies and not so easily put off. However, as anyone knows who's worked at council election level with supporters who are much less committed and who perhaps just deliver a few leaflets in their own road, forgetting to thank them afterwards can lead to a decimation of delivery workers next time round. Why else do we all hold post-election 'thank you parties' nowadays?

The truth is, no one ever minds being thanked, and it is, when all's said and done, as much as anything a mark of good manners. However, being thanked in person by the candidate and having one's hand shaken *fifty years to the day* after the by-election at which one helped may possibly be some sort of record. As is the postcard shown hereunder, received on 4 April 2012:

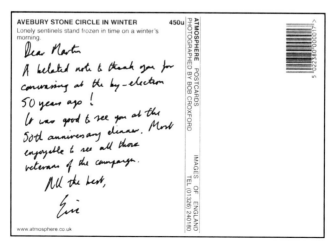

APPENDIX 1:

Southampton wards 1959-65
contested by Liberal candidates

All figures are taken from the files of press cuttings of the *Daily Echo* held by Southampton Central Library, to whose staff the author is obliged for their generous assistance.

During the period covered by this volume, Southampton City Council consisted of 18 wards:

Ward	1959	1960	1961	1962	1963	1964	1965
Banister	•	•	•	✓	•	•	•
Bargate	•	•	•	✓	•	•	•
Bassett	•	•	•	•	•	•	•
Bitterne	•	•	•	✓	✓	✓	✓
Coxford	•	•	•	✓	✓	•	•
Freemantle	✓	✓	✓	✓	✓	✓	•
Harefield	•	•	•	•	•	•	✓
Millbrook	✓	✓	✓	✓	✓	✓	•
Pear Tree & Bitterne Manor	•	•	•	•	✓	✓	✓
Portswood	•	•	✓	✓	✓	✓	✓
Redbridge	•	•	•	•	•	•	•
St Denys & Bitterne Park	•	•	•	✓	✓	✓	✓
St Luke's	✓	✓	•	•	✓	✓	✓
St Mary's	•	•	•	•	•	•	•
Shirley	•	•	•	✓	✓	✓	•
Sholing	•	•	•	•	•	•	•
Swaythling	•	•	•	✓	✓	✓	✓
Woolston	•	✓	•	•	✓	✓	✓
Total number of Liberal candidates	3	4	3	10	11	10	8
Number of second places	0	0	1	3	0	0	0

1959

Freemantle

Candidate	Party	Votes
A. Guard	Lab	1 321
T. Eccles	Con-RP	1 186
L. Burke	Lib	314
	Maj	135

Millbrook

Candidate	Party	Votes
A. Reynard	Lab	1 762
J. Motyer	Con-RP	1 639
M. White*	Lib	635
	Maj	123

Lab gain

St Luke's

Candidate	Party	Votes
J. Young	Con-RP	1 674
Mrs Sager	Lab	1 603
G. Payne	Lib	397
	Maj	71

Woolston

By-election 30 December 1959

Candidate	Party	Votes
A. O'Rourke	Lab	970
Mrs J. Breton	Con-RP	814
L. Burke	Lib	264
	Maj	156

1960

Freemantle

Candidate	Party	Votes
T. Eccles	Con-RP	1 177
L. Goater	Lab	1 020
L. Burke	Lib	524
	Maj	157

Millbrook

Candidate	Party	Votes
R. Baker	Con-RP	1 743
A. Moon	Lab	1 578
M. White	Lib	778
	Maj	167

Con-RP gain

St Luke's

Candidate	Party	Votes
J. Adams	Con-RP	1 478
D. Barnes	Lab	1 335
G. Payne	Lib	380
	Maj	143

Con-RP gain

Woolston

Candidate	Party	Votes
F. McManus	Lab	1 461
Mrs King	Con-RP	1 373
F. Bradley	Lib	326
	Maj	88

1961

Freemantle

Candidate	Party	Votes
L. Goater	Lab	1 105
R. Maunder	Con-RP	1 075
L. Burke	Lib	608
	Maj	30

Millbrook

Candidate	Party	Votes
W. Cook	Con-RP	1 720
R. Russell	Lab	1 627
M. White	Lib	976
	Maj	93

Con-RP gain

St Luke's

No Liberal candidate

Woolston

No Liberal candidate

* Mark White's family came from the Channel Islands, which may account for his full name being Marcel Fred Jean White.

1959
Portswood

No Liberal candidate

1962
Freemantle

A. Guard	Lab	1 160
E. Blow	Con-RP	832
L. Burke	Lib	790
	Maj	328

1962
Millbrook

A. Reynard	Lab	1 648
G. Southwell*	Lib	1 353
Mrs Pugh	Con-RP	1 281
	Maj	295

1962
St Luke's

No Liberal candidate

1960
Portswood

No Liberal candidate

1963
Freemantle

R. Mundy	Lab	1 151
T. Eccles	Con-RP	908
L. Burke	Lib	448
Lab gain	*Maj*	243

1963
Millbrook

C. Smith	Lab	1 773
R. Baker	Con-RP	1 334
G. Southwell	Lib	1 004
Lab gain	*Maj*	439

1963
St Luke's

E. Clark	Lab	1 378
J. Adams	Con-RP	1 171
Mrs M. Kyrle	Lib	559
J. Bonnin	Com	64
Lab gain	*Maj*	207

1961
Portswood

J. Barr	Con-RP	2 081
P. Leigh	Lib	659
Mrs Mills	Lab	591
	Maj	1 422

1964
Freemantle

L. Goater	Lab	1 292
T. Eccles	Con-RP	965
E. Lamb	Lib	203
	Maj	327

1964
Millbrook

R. Smith	Lab	1 900
W. Cook	Con-RP	1 588
G. Southwell	Lib	439
Lab gain	*Maj*	312

1964
St Luke's

H. Brett	Lab	1 470
T. Heys	Con-RP	1 177
D. Brooks	Lib	448
Lab gain	*Maj*	293

* Gordon Southwell found campaigning very difficult because he was a baker by trade and had to get up each morning at 3 o'clock to go to work.

1962
Woolston

No Liberal candidate

1963
Woolston

J. Watkins	Lab	1 886
J. Burns	Con-RP	1 048
Miss Lodge	Lib	532
P. Ware	Com	93
	Maj	838

1964
Woolston

Mrs Cooper	Lab	1 969
J. Burns	Con-RP	1 049
Miss Lodge	Lib	328
P. Ware	Com	73
	Maj	920

1962
Portswood

S. Royl	Con-RP	1 737
P. Leigh	**Lib**	**866**
Mrs Sager	Lab	783
	Maj	871

1963
Portswood

A. Mitchell	Con-RP	1 798
C. Seyd	Lab	919
R. Withers	Lib	477
	Maj	879

1964
Portswood

J. Barr	Con-RP	1 858
R. Kneller	Lab	879
M. Fiddes	Lib	653
	Maj	979

1962
Bitterne

J. Austin	Lab	2 784
E. King	Con-RP	2 008
D. Trotman	Lib	983
A. Pearse	Com	107
Lab gain	*Maj*	776

1963
Bitterne

F. McManus	Lab	2 625
F. Childs	Con-RP	1 964
M. Fiddes	Lib	493
A. Pearse	Com	103
	Maj	664

1965
Freemantle

No Liberal candidate

1965
Millbrook

No Liberal candidate

1962

Coxford

L. Squibb	Lab	2 689
A. Wales	Con-RP	859
A. Sparkes	Lib	544
R. Shannon	Com	80
	Maj	1 830

Pear Tree & Bitterne Manor

No Liberal candidate

St Denys & Bitterne Park

W. Osborne	Con-RP	1 359
J. Walter	Lab	1 300
A. Millard	Lib	814
	Maj	59

Shirley

R. Stewart	Con-RP	2 101
B. Baxter†	**Lib**	**933**
Mrs Holdup	Lab	734
	Maj	1 168

1963

Coxford

R. McGuirk*	Lab	2 559
Mrs Ingle	Con-RP	908
R. Marks	Lib	335
R. Shannon	Com	49
	Maj	1 651

Pear Tree & Bitterne Manor

Mrs Sager	Lab	2 118
A. Wookey	Con-RP	1 485
E. Humby	Lib	705
Lab gain	*Maj*	633

St Denys & Bitterne Park

D. Martin	Con-RP	1 394
J. Walter	Lab	1 370
A. Millard	Lib	494
	Maj	24

Shirley

J. Dawson	Con-RP	2 078
Mrs Holdup	Lab	767
L. Mockett	Lib	541
	Maj	1 311

1965

St Luke's

J. Adams	Con-RP	1 311
R. Carter	Lab	1098
A. Millard	Lib	370
Con-RP gain	*Maj*	213

Woolston

J. Hardie	Lab	1 398
C. Mitchell	Con-RP	1 225
Mrs Smith	Lib	173
P. Ware	Com	71
	Maj	173

Portswood

W. Head	Con-RP	2 157
Mrs O'Beirne	Lab	678
Mrs Daniels	Lib	471
	Maj	1 479

* At a time of full employment, if anyone was without a job it was seen as due to their own shortcomings, i.e. they were probably unemployable. As Mr McGuirk was unemployed we wondered how he could afford to be on the council when, remember, councillors were not paid. Amongst ourelves in private he was known as 'Out-of-work McGuirk'.

† Benny Baxter assured us that if he got elected his first priority would be to sell the piano in the Civic Centre and use the money to subsidise old people's lunches.

1962
Swaythling

F. Halfpenny	Lab	1 865
M. Flynn	Con-RP	757
W. Symmons	Lib	595
T. Gibbs	Com	45
	Maj	1 108

1962
Banister

H. Cole	Con-RP	1 468
D. Bull	Lab	555
R. Withers	Lib	509
	Maj	913

1962
Bargate

G. Scriven	Lab	1 283
J. Humphreys	Con-RP	935
R. Marks	Lib	329
	Maj	348

1963
Swaythling

Mrs Williams	Lab	1 769
M. Goodwin	Con-RP	753
H. Avery	Lib	450
Mrs Maleski	Com	40
	Maj	1 016

1963
Banister

No Liberal candidate

1963
Bargate

No Liberal candidate

1964
Bitterne

S. Baker	Lab	2 723
M. Wilkins	Lab	2 545
M. Pettet	Con-RP	2 101
F. Childs	Con-RP	2 084
J. Austin	Lib	379
F. Whelan	Lib	288
A. Pearse	Com	150
One Lab gain	*Maj*	622

1965
Bitterne

M. Pettet	Con-RP	2 216
M. Wilkins	Lab	1 795
Mrs Clark	Lib	413
Con-RP gain	*Maj*	421

1964
Harefield

No Liberal candidate

1965
Harefield

A. Jenkins	Con-RP	1 540
Mrs Fowler	Lab	1 137
Mrs de Souza	Lib	538
Con-RP gain	*Maj*	403

1964
Pear Tree & Bitterne Manor

D. Speake	Lab	2 215
A. Wookey	Con-RP	1 524
E. Humby	Lib	439
	Maj	691

1965
Pear Tree & Bitterne Manor

L. Gulliford	Lab	1 635
A. Shotter	Con-RP	1 615
B. Maisey	Lib	485
	Maj	20

1964
St Denys & Bitterne Park

L. Crabb	Con-RP	1 628
E. Eaborn	Lab	1 411
D. Parker	Lib	284
	Maj	217

1965
St Denys & Bitterne Park

W. Osborne	Con-RP	1 686
R. Kneller	Lab	1 056
D. Parker	Lib	291
	Maj	630

THE ALDERMANIC BY-ELECTIONS, JUNE 1961

(v. page 65)

Bassett

W. Johnson	Con-RP	1 870
J. Watkins	Lab	1 266
	Maj	604

Portswood

S. Royl	Con-RP	1 391
P. Leigh	Lib	691
	Maj	700

Shirley

J. Dawson	Con-RP	1 777
G. Barnes	Con-RP	1 754
Mrs M. Kyrle	Lib	378
A. Pratt	Lib	325
T. Gibbs	Comm	63
R. Shannon	Comm	25
	Maj	1 399

APPENDIX 2

A GOOD READ – WITH A DIFFERENCE !

Martin Kyrle's
Little Green Nightbook

Martin Kyrle's *Little Green Nightbook* is a distillation of fireside yarns from his travels – around the country, around the continent and occasionally beyond – during half a century.

Written in the first person and in a conversational style, these light-hearted recollections touch on the lasting legacies of national service and university student days at Southampton in the 1950s and Sussex in the '60s. They range over unexpected encounters with people or fate when – *inter alia* – travelling independently behind the Iron Curtain, chancing his arm hitchhiking in Lapland, left-hand driving in the rush hour in Granada, having a suspected heart attack on a cross-Channel ferry and extricating himself and his wife from a village church in Devon after being locked in.

They are tales of 'adventure' in the Chaucerian sense of '*by aventure y-falle*'. Funny things can happen - and did! - in places where you'd least expect them, and his deliberately individualistic choice of words draws you into the scene and makes you feel as though you're watching from a front row seat. Then there are some of the characters he met on the road or in youth hostels who had extraordinary stories to tell which are well worth passing on. Other tales describe predicaments which invite the challenge 'Now get out of *that*!', and you find out how he managed, often well off the beaten track and, of course, long before mobile phones were invented.

The author sets out merely to divert and entertain, but stories which revolve around, for example, working in post-World War II refugee camps in Austria, in a home for mentally handicapped children in Worcestershire and taking school parties to Scandinavia or the Low Countries present a snapshot of times very different from our own.

Illustrations and front cover by Derek Snowdon

Perfect bound, 212pp, ISBN 978-0-9364791-3-3

£8.95

Enquiries: 16 Park Road, Chandler's Ford, Eastleigh, Hants SO53 2EU or E: martinkyrle@fsmail.net

Printed and published by Sarsen Press, 22 Hyde St., Winchester SO23 7DR

*Each copy comes with a **free** elastic band!*

- -

ORDERS

I enclose cheque (payable to "M. Kyrle") for £............   Please supply a copy to the following:

Name: ....

Address:...Postcode................

If to be posted please add: inland 2nd class £1.40, 1st class £1.60,
Europe £4.22, or world-wide: surface £4.21, air £6.98

Martin Kyrle's

LITTLE GREEN

NIGHTBOOK

is a distillation of fireside yarns
from his travels – around the
country, around the continent
and occasionally beyond
– during half a century

INTRODUCTION **A**

Not to be
opened until
tomorrow

Do Not Browse
To find out why, turn to the back cover

Written in the first person, these stories are designed to be read in bed just before you go to sleep. The way to enjoy this book is to follow the author's intentions: read one letter each night, put in your bookmark, firmly resist the temptation to turn the page and read the next one, switch off the bedside light and go to sleep. That way you have nighttime reading – hence the book's title – for a month, more or less, and at quiet moments during the course of each day you can, if you so fancy, speculate about what'll be on the reading menu tonight: which country you'll be transported to, and whether he'll be telling you about something which happened to him last year or half a century ago. To read it straight through would be the equivalent of ordering a three-course meal of, say, tomato soup, poached salmon with a side salad followed by chocolate fudge cake with hot sauce – and then putting them all on the same plate and eating the mixture with a spoon. Of course, it's a free country. But courses are served separately so that different flavours may be enjoyed.